Edwin Muir

Edwin Muir

a master of modern poetry

MICHAEL J. PHILLIPS

HACKETT PUBLISHING COMPANY, INC.

Indianapolis · Cambridge

EDWIN MUIR: 1887–1959

Copyright © 1978 by Michael J. Phillips
All rights reserved
Book design by James N. Rogers
Printed in the United States of America
First Printing

Library of Congress Catalog Card Number: 78–67103
ISBN Number: 0–915144–54–9

For further information, please address
Hackett Publishing Company, Inc., Box 55573,
Indianapolis, Indiana 46205

ABOUT THE AUTHOR...

Poet-author Michael J. Phillips is a native of Indianapolis, where he currently resides. He received his M.A. degree in Letters from Indiana University and his doctorate in Comparative Literature from Purdue University, Phi Beta Kappa. In 1969, he was a Practice Teacher at Oxford University, and a Visiting Fellow at Harvard University, 1976–77. His poetry has been widely published in magazines, folios, and books, and has been delivered in public readings, dramatic presentations, recordings, and in shows. His most recent collection, *Visual Poems*, appeared in 1976.

CONTENTS

I

Introduction

The Scottish poet Edwin Muir did not command a large, educated literary public in his own lifetime as the more formally educated Ezra Pound and T. S. Eliot did. He did not become a left-wing spokesman in poetry for the decade whose intelligentsia was leaning toward Marxism and socialism, as was the case with English poets of the thirties. He did not strike a dominantly rational sexual romantic note as Robert Graves was to do. He did not exemplify the ideal of how poetry should be both read and written in combination with phonographic recording, an achievement that was to belong to Dylan Thomas. There were few voices asserting his greatness when he was alive, while many proclaimed the classical stature of William Butler Yeats and, in America, Robert Frost. He did not captivate the youth of a whole decade, as Allen Ginsberg was to do in the 1960s in the U.S.A. He came too early to be tempted by Continental movements in the sixties such as concrete poetry, alphabetism, kinetic poetry, spatialism, sound poetry, abstract poetry, or minimal art. Instead, as a quiet poet of high quality, Muir has gradually established himself and has been more appreciated in the seventies than earlier, providing in his work an alternative or complement to the usual offerings of many courses in modern British poetry.

Against the background of what one might call "reserved poetry" in an "Age of Reserve"—the second third of the twentieth century (Dylan Thomas is the notable exception)—Muir painstakingly and gently wrought, in the style of his maturity, the poems (later called "mythological structures") which would gradually prove appealing, significant, and enduring to generations of readers. More and more versifiers, students, and followers of poetry have written and spoken about him with the passage of time, during the fifties and sixties in Great Britain, Italy, the United States, and France. As the quantity of reviews, articles, and books increased, the quality of his reputation gradually became commensurate with the quality of the poems.

Muir's life is well documented in his own *The Story and the Fable*[1] and *An Autobiography;*[2] Willa Muir's *Belonging*[3] and Peter Butter's *Edwin Muir: Man and Poet*[4] provide further information. Born on May 15, 1887, and dying on January 3, 1959, he lived a comparatively active, cosmopolitan life. The poet was a voracious reader at nine, and he had little schooling after his fourteenth birthday. He relied on friends and groups of friends (usually in Glasgow) in combination with his own reading for his earlier higher education. He had many occupations in the course of a busy set of careers—he worked as clerk, laborer, journalist, reviewer, editor, translator, administrator, and teacher down through the decades. He had been out in the world, virtually alone, for fifteen years, before he started publishing. For the most part, either Muir or his wife had to work and earn a living to create the leisure necessary for him to realize his artistic ambitions. His experience with many vocations and many aspects of life, as he went on, created a means by which he could share in varying experiences of the world. Both as a man and as a poet, he might be called a "superrealist."

He was known among his friends and acquaintances as having a special "saintlike" quality. Perhaps the broad experience with many facets of Glasgow (his home before turning to writing) and then his cosmopolitanism throughout his long life engendered the special kindness that Muir was noted for. The humble quality of the man must have created the radiance that surrounded him—his unassuming modesty and quietness of voice enhanced his every action. Along with these traits was the attribute of determination supporting an enduring ambition to succeed as a poet. Working in the man was one other principal characteristic (perhaps the most notable of all): a certain admiration and respect for his fellow human beings. This seems to be lacking in many modern writers—as well as many modern people. It comes out in poems like "The Visitor" and "One Foot in Eden":

The Visitor

No, no, do not beguile me, do not come
Between me and my ghost, that cannot move
Till you are gone,

1. Edwin Muir, *The Story and the Fable* (London: Harrap, 1940). Hereafter, when the title only of a work is cited, the reader may assume the author to be Edwin Muir.

2. *An Autobiography* (London: Methuen, 1968).

3. Willa Muir, *Belonging* (London: Hogarth, 1968).

4. Peter Butter, *Edwin Muir: Man and Poet* (Edinburgh: Oliver, 1966).

And while you gossip must be dumb.
Do not believe I do not want your love,
Brother and sister, wife and son.
But I would be alone
Now, now and let him in,
Lest while I speak he is already flown,
Offended by the din
Of this half-uttered scarcely whispered plea
(So delicate is he).
No more, no more.
Let the great tidings stay unsaid,
For I must to the door,
And oh I dread
He may even now be gone
Or, when I open, will not enter in.[5]

One Foot in Eden

One foot in Eden still, I stand
And look across the other land.
The world's great day is growing late,
Yet strange these fields that we have planted
So long with crops of love and hate.
Time's handiworks by time are haunted,
And nothing now can separate
The corn and tares compactly grown.
The armorial weed in stillness bound
About the stalk; these are our own.
Evil and good stand thick around
In the fields of charity and sin
Where we shall lead our harvest in.

Yet still from Eden springs the root
As clean as on the starting day.
Time takes the foliage and the fruit
And burns the archetypal leaf
To shapes of terror and of grief
Scattered along the winter way.
But famished field and blackened tree
Bear flowers in Eden never known.

5. "The Visitor," p. 198. All subsequent page citations for poems refer to works appearing in Muir's *Collected Poems* (New York: Oxford University Press, 1965).

Blossoms of grief and charity
Bloom in these darkened fields alone.
What had Eden ever to say
Of hope and faith and pity and love
Until was buried all its day
And memory found its treasure trove?
Strange blessings never in Paradise
Fall from these beclouded skies.[6]

Muir spoke and wrote poetry sensitively, softly, and also in stately, proces-
sional fashion; yet he wrote with perspicuity. Always, there is adequate
moral perspective. The voice we hear in these poems—as well as the repro-
duction of Muir's reading that we can hear on his Library of Congress tape
recording[7]—is that of a fundamentally good man, a person with sound
common sense who was aware of virtue in the world around him.

Another fine quality of the man should be mentioned separately. Extension of the imagination to reality or unrealities in the manufacture of a
poem requires an individual who has a capacity for bravery as well as bold-
ness. This hard-grained quality of Muir is particularly important if we keep
in mind the important points that Muir raised about reality in *An Autobiography:*

Our minds are possessed by three mysteries: where we came
from, where we are going, and, since we are not alone, but members of a countless family, how we should live with one another.[8]

Muir examined these mysteries throughout his life; the probing and questioning is characteristic of all the poems. Perhaps raising such fundamental
concerns had something to do with his psychological problems—problems
that he transcended. For the most part, he lived with full consciousness of
the tensions that exist between what we know of life or reality and what
we feel it should be. The awareness of too much evil in a world that is
also good raises questions and produces anxiety. Muir was not alone in this
sense of mystery and concern as to what life is about, how it could be
explained, or how one dealt with its horrible, particular aspects in the twentieth century. He managed to avoid a permanently debilitating breakdown,

6. "One Foot in Eden," p. 227.

7. *Twentieth Century Poetry in English* (Washington, D.C.: Library of Congress, 1955).

8. *An Autobiography,* p. 56.

and, for the greater part of his life, enjoyed good mental health. A leggy, unsentimental stance in metaphysics requires toughness and wisdom, in the presence of the everyday realities that all perceptive human beings face. The sinewy quality of Muir in the face of the open universe is apparent in a comment made upon a children's life of Jesus, which his mother read to him:

> It must have been written in a vein of mawkish sentiment, for it gave me the impression that Jesus was always slightly ill, a pale invalid with the special gentleness of people who cannot live as others do.[9]

He was an expert conversationalist, an adroit thinker, and a compelling and popular teacher—in short, a highly brilliant and knowledgeable human being (as well as a good one), in spite of his lack of formal education. This quality of intellect can be seen in any of the earlier writings which demonstrate a profound reflective capacity as they deal with abstract ideas, but particularly the early semiphilosophical essays published in the *New Age* from 1913 to 1924[10] and the *Freeman* from 1920 to 1924.[11] Muir was able to write at the age of thirty-five:

> Up to a century or two ago, the ruling ideas of men were given by religion, and these ideas given by religion were not only religious ideas, and therefore eternal and to be felt by some men into whatever time they may happen to be born; they were ideas on government, on commerce, on life in this world and on the constitution of the universe. This second class of ideas has, whether we welcome the fact or not, been gradually disintegrating, and is now without any effective power. And there has been no central conception to replace it. We have had no fundamental conviction about government, about commerce, or about life, but, on the contrary, a score of theories, none of which comes home to our bosoms. The result is that specialism has knocked life out of proportion, and in doing that has made it intellectually unmanageable. We have still to work out our ideas in fear and trembling, and with these perhaps our salvation.[12]

9. Ibid., p. 28.

10. Listed in Elgin Mellown, *Bibliography of the Writings of Edwin Muir*, pp. 55–69.

11. Ibid., pp. 61–69.

12. "Labour's Statistical Boa-Constrictor," *New Age* 12 (12 October 1922), p. 298.

He had prepared himself to think brilliantly in what is called "the prime of life." The philosophical bent of Muir's mind was always showing up in the poems as he matured as an artist, and his talent for intelligent reflection on literature accompanied his writing of verse through the years. It is, however, in the early essays, and then later, just three years before his death, in the Norton Lectures delivered at Harvard,[13] that Muir is most manifest as a practicing and theoretical critic. A certain practical direction in his criticism had been evident in the intervening 35 years—the period when Muir went through a lengthy period of development that helped to create the best poems which appear in the final *Collected Poems*.

The basic process of probing and questioning, typical of Muir's mind, and its fruition in rational skeptical thought (already touched on in connection with his theorizing as he dealt with man's ideological and religious systems) is evident in an essay, "The Truth About Art" (published in the *Freeman*), that I wish to consider in relation to late statements in *The Estate Of Poetry*. The questions of a secular and independent man of the twentieth century take on a highly Promethean quality in the former essay:

> What if all the assumptions on which we have thus far judged art should be—erroneous? What if every system of aesthetics and every criticism should be, not merely wrong here and there, but by their very existence the standing, immemorial misunderstanding of art? In short, what if questions regarding the function and the "meaning" of art simply should not be asked at all, and, in any case, should never be answered?[14]

This early capacity for agonizing introspection and intelligent interrogation (very characteristic of Muir in his late thirties) was to pay off in answer to his questions 33 years later at Harvard in 1955 in the realm of literary speculation when he could say that

> poetry too has its object, which is not knowledge in the scientific or philosophical sense, but the creation of a true image of life. We all help to create that image, for imagination is a faculty as natural to us as the desire to see and to know.[15]

Not satisfied with merely creating an excellent statement as to the proper

13. *The Estate of Poetry* (Boston: Harvard University Press, 1962).

14. "The Truth about Art," *Freeman* 4 (15 February 1922), p. 537.

15. *The Estate of Poetry*, pp. 107–108.

object of poetry, Muir goes on in an even more probing vein, and makes a high claim for poetry in our lives:

> Without it we would not understand one another, or make friends, or fall in love, or know what love and friendship and life are. The supreme expression of imagination is in poetry, and so like philosophy and science it has a responsibility to itself: the responsibility to preserve a true image of life. If the image is true, poetry fulfills its end. Anything that distorts the image, any tendency to oversimplify or soften it so that it may be more acceptable to a greater number of people, falsifies it, degrades those for whom it is intended, and cannot set us free. This means that the first allegiance of any poet is to imaginative truth, and that if he is to serve mankind, that is the only way in which he can do it.[16]

One can think of Muir asking a fundamental question about art and criticism (as evidenced in the 1922 statement in the *Freeman*); achieving, in his later years, a partial reconciliation with the human order; then filling up some of the gaps that existed for him. His own poetry, no doubt, loomed as central and significant in making the jump from aesthetic and philosophical pessimism to artistic truth without abandoning philosophy. Speaking of one realm of poetry—the imaginative realm—Muir says:

> You may say that by cultivating his holding each poet adds to the world of poetic imagination, and that therefore it can never be regarded as completely embodied—reason for discouragement and hope, and an earnest of the continuance of poetry.[17]

The assumptions of criticism and aesthetics that the poet attacked in the *Freeman* have here been replaced, in *The Estate of Poetry*, by the poet's own views. Muir's earlier questioning meant that he could create the independence necessary to maintain a quality of individuation and detachment. A certain reluctance to accept things has been a necessary concomitant to the generation, birth, and growth of original art and the description of that art in philosophical language. At the age of sixty-eight, Muir had come a long way from a culture where there were obvious limitations:

16. Ibid., p. 108.

17. Ibid., p. 1.

> In our farmhouse in one of the smaller Orkney islands,
> there were not many books apart from the Bible, *The Pilgrim's
> Progress*, and the poems of Burns.[18]

Obviously there were virtues too, since Muir learned to write great poetry.

Muir's view of his own life, as documented in *The Story and the Fable*, is characterized by two central tendencies: movement of the sensibility outward, toward apprehension of the external world, and a movement inward toward apprehension of the internal world or the world of imagination. In terms of external sensibility, the distinction between "the story" and "the fable" no doubt played a large part in the composition of the autobiography. Scenes from the environment take on a fabulous dimension, as when Muir is speaking of his parents:

> But I cannot bring back my mental impression of them, for
> it is overlaid by later memories in which I saw them as a man
> and a woman, like, or almost like, other men and women. I am
> certain that I did not see them like this at first; I never thought
> that they were like other men and women; to me they were
> fixed allegorical figures in a timeless landscape. Their allegorical
> changelessness made them more, not less, solid, as if they were
> condensed into something more real than humanity; as if the
> image 'mother' meant more than 'woman,' and the image 'father'
> more than 'man.'[19]

The plain "man" or the "woman" may be thought of as "the story," whereas their special human qualities and the fact of their being Muir's parents are the points where the "man" and "woman" become (1) special or (2) "mother" or "father"; or to put it another way, the points at which the "story" becomes "fable"—becomes fabulous. It is the point where reality takes on a significant meaning, if one has the proper and correct way of looking at it. Muir takes dreams very seriously throughout this work; shifting from the realm of external reality to an inward sphere, Muir likewise supplies a criterion for looking at life itself after discussing the way that a memory of a dream has worked on "the unresolved questions of our past"[20] in such a way as to work out or solve a lingering problem. In this particular case an act of cowardliness in childhood with respect to a fight is

18. Ibid., p. 9.

19. *The Story and the Fable*, p. 25

20. Ibid., p. 48.

solved in a poem that comes to terms with the myth of Hector and
Achilles:

> And in that space our shadows run,
>   His shadow there and mine,
> The little flowers, the tiny mounds,
> The grasses frail and fine.[21]

Here we have a situation where the "superreal" compensates for the "real"
through our consciousness ·of the Platonic doctrine of shadows that is
embodied in the poem. If our conscious faculties (those we use in writing
the poem) resolve a particular situation, then this fact suggests that life has
a meaning:

> These solutions of the past projected into the present, deliber-
> ately announced as if they were a sibylline declaration that life
> has a meaning, impress me more deeply than any other kind of
> experience with the conviction that life does have a meaning
> quite apart from the thousand meanings which the conscious
> mind attributes to it: an unexpected and yet incontestable
> meaning which runs in the teeth of ordinary experience, per-
> fectly coherent, yet depending on a different system of con-
> nected relations from that by which we consciously live.[22]

Whether looking to the external world, or looking to a process in subconscious life, Muir perceives the "fable" as going along with the "story."
There is nothing sentimental or arbitrary about the fable, for Muir; it is
what orients the story.

> It is clear that no autobiography can begin with a man's birth,
> that we extend far beyond any boundary line which we can set
> for ourselves in the past or the future.[23]

Thus, by 1940, the idea of extension that is so important in the later
poems—whether it be reaching backward in the past, centering in on a
moment-to-moment existence, or moving toward an understanding of the
future—is established here. The idea of movement in time is coupled with
the modest question:

21. "Ballad of Hector in Hades," pp. 24–26.

22. *The Story and the Fable*, p. 49.

23. Ibid., p. 54.

how can he [man] know himself? I am writing about myself in
this book, yet I do not know what I am. I know my name, the
date and place of my birth, the appearance of the places I have
lived in, the people I have met, the things I have done.[24]

These realms of places, people, and action were to concern Muir more
and more as he approached death. It is the interplay between the "story"
and the "fable," the question of summing up a life with adequate account
of man's relation to time, and the probings of the mystery of life itself that
make *The Story and the Fable* such a welcome addition to twentieth-
century autobiography.

The principal difference between *The Story and the Fable* and *An
Autobiography* (the latter published fourteen years later, in 1954) springs
from the addition of 87 pages, containing Muir's account of his own life up
to and through the war years, the second stay in Prague, and later the
years in Rome, Great Britain, America, and Scotland. Chapter VII ("Extracts
from a Diary, 1937–39") is dropped. Muir must have felt that the continuity of the narrative would be interrupted by inclusion of the "Dream
Diary" (the diary is composed principally of dreams and provides a partial
record of Muir's subconscious in the period from 1937 to 1939).[25] An element of nostalgia for his birthplace comes out in the pages written by the
older man:

> I do not know whether in others the impressions of the first
> seven years of their lives remain so vivid and lasting, or if it is
> good that they should. In any case we need a symbolical stage
> on which the drama of human life can play itself out for us, and
> I doubt whether we have the liberty to choose it.[26]

Besides keeping in mind that Muir had lived through two world wars, one
ought to remember that the poet's life just before and during the years in
Glasgow was characterized by near poverty; the loss of his mother, father,
and two brothers (all within five years of his nineteenth birthday); poor
living conditions; and shabby, uncomfortable jobs. Consequently, the
earlier, happy years in Orkney take on an added significance.

Muir focuses on problems of evil as he considers some of the atrocities
in the Second World War:

24. Ibid., p. 55.

25. Ibid., pp. 237–264.

26. *An Autobiography*, p. 206.

Evil works itself out from generation to generation, but to observe it happening, to be confronted with one particular illustration of the universal law, is like a violation of the ordinary faith which makes us believe that all men can be saved.[27]

Perhaps this particular "shock of recognition," as well as Muir's more general historical sense, led him to create *The Story and the Fable* and *An Autobiography*. In a way these pages are vitiated by the question of whether life has a meaning or not. Autobiography is one way of approaching the answer to this question. It would appear that Muir sees some concrete evidence of such meaning, as he sums up his own experience:

I have written this continuation of my autobiography at Newbattle, in scraps of spare time and during vacations. What is left to say when one has come to the end of writing about one's life? Some kind of development, I suppose, should be expected to emerge, but I am very doubtful of such things, for I cannot bring life into a neat pattern. If there is a development in my life—and that seems an idle supposition—then it has been brought about more by things outside than by any conscious intention of my own. I was lucky to spend my first fourteen years in Orkney; I was unlucky to live afterwards in Glasgow as a Displaced Person, until at last I acquired a liking for that plain, warm-hearted city. Because a perambulating revivalist preacher came to Kirkwall when I was a boy, I underwent an equivocal religious conversion there; because I read Blatchford in Glasgow, I repeated the experience in another form, and found myself a Socialist. In my late twenties I came, by chance, under the influence of Nietzsche. In my early thirties I had the good fortune to meet my wife, and have had since the greater good fortune of sharing my life with her. In my middle thirties I became aware of immortality, and realized that it gave me a truer knowledge of myself and my neighbours. Years later in St. Andrews I discovered that I had been a Christian without knowing it. I saw in Czechoslovakia a whole people lost by one of the cruel turns of history, and exiled from themselves in the heart of their own country. I discovered in Italy that Christ had walked on the earth, and also that things truly made preserve themselves through time in the first freshness of their nature.

27. Ibid., p. 262.

Now and then during these years I fell into the dumps for short
or prolonged periods, was subject to fears which I did not understand, and passed through stretches of blankness and deprivation.
From these I learned things which I could not otherwise have
learned, so that I cannot regard them as mere loss. Yet I believe
that I would have been better without them.

When we talk of our development I fancy we mean little
more than that we have changed with the changing world; and if
we are writers or intellectuals, that our ideas have changed with
the changing fashions of thought, and therefore not always for
the better. I think that if any of us examines his life, he will find
that most good has come to him from a few loyalties, and a few
discoveries made many generations before he was born, which
must always be made anew. These too may sometimes appear to
come by chance, but in the infinite web of things and events
chance must be something different from what we think it to be.
To comprehend that is not given to us, and to think of it is to
recognize a mystery, and to acknowledge the necessity of faith.
As I look back on the part of the mystery which is my own life,
my own fable, what I am most aware of is that we receive more
than we can ever give; we receive it from the past, on which we
draw with every breath, but also—and this is a point of faith—
from the Source of the mystery itself, by the means which
religious people call Grace.[28]

Muir spoke warmly of his marriage: "My marriage was the most fortunate event in my life."[29] In *Belonging*, Willa Muir, Edwin's wife, added to
the documentation of his life shortly after his death: more than most wives,
she had added to his life—particularly as a helpmate in the translations, and
as a wage earner. *Belonging* is a book on an equal level with *The Story
and the Fable* and *An Autobiography*, and, in a modest way, an impres-
sive tribute. It suggests that a vital intimacy existed between the pair.
Mrs. Muir's account and style are much like Muir's. The memories pertaining to their courtship suggest the feminine warmth and closeness that must
have been welcomed by Muir through all his life in spite of the relationship's "impropitious beginnings", as described by his wife:

I first met Edwin Muir in a Glasgow flat sometime during

28. Ibid., pp. 280–281.

29. Ibid., p. 154.

September 1918. On the face of things our meeting was unlikely; he was a costing-clerk in a Renfrew shipbuilding firm and I was a lecturer in a London training college for teachers. It was still more unlikely that having met we should get married less than a year later and most unlikely of all that our marriage should last.[30]

The actual meeting and introduction are charmingly depicted and suggest sources for the spontaneous warmth the schoolteacher felt before the author of a book who was also a white-collar worker:

But when he came in and was introduced the labels fell off at once. As I usually did when meeting young men for the first time, I looked at eyes and mouth. I had too often met well-shaped foreheads and clever eyes spoilt by ill-shaped mouths, tight-lipped or foolish, the mouths of men whose intellects had been educated but not their feelings. Edwin Muir's eyes and mouth promised well; his brow was an intellectual's, disproportionately wide and high, very noticeable above the slight, even meagre body, yet his eyes were dreamy-looking, sea-blue, with a hint of distance in them, and his mouth was well cut, with full, sensitive lips. A little later I noticed that one of his thin shoulders, the left, as if cramped with too much leaning on an elbow, was held stiffly above the level of the other. But when he laughed two blue flashes shot from his eyes and one forgot the cramped shoulder. His voice, too, was pleasantly soft and gentle.[31]

Edwin and Willa met soon thereafter again:

The floor was good and our steps matched so well that we floated rather than danced round the hall. I had never had so light-footed a partner, nor, perhaps, had he, for as the evening wore on it became understood between us that we should partner each other for all the waltzes. As the evening wore on, too, we became more and more wordless.[32]

In retrospect, Mrs. Muir writes of the experience and the sense of "belonging"—the idea she was to use as her title:

30. Willa Muir, *Belonging*, p. 11.

31. Ibid., p. 15

32. Ibid., p. 22.

> The feeling which rose up and overwhelmed me that evening,
> obliterating my conscious self, was like the feeling of Belonging
> to the Universe but stronger, even more joyous, more full of
> wonder. It seemed inexhaustible. I suspect that Edwin was having
> the same experience, for we inherited, each of us, a primitive
> simplicity from our Orkney and Shetland forebears which was
> likely to be wide open to vibrations from our tribal uncon-
> scious.[33]

Her description of this set of experiences suggests one thing: that Willa
Muir had a firm and secure romantic basis in her feeling for Edwin.

Love is, to a certain extent, a myth made by oneself and by others. It is
also a genuine, fundamental, and individual reality for most people. In this
case, as in the Muirs' lives, one is struck by the strength, selectiveness,
quality, and value of their lifelong relationship with each other.

Peter Butter, professor of English at Glasgow University and author of
the first book-length critical work on Edwin Muir,[34] adds to the story left
by Willa and Edwin Muir in a book he wrote four years later, the bio-
graphical *Edwin Muir: Man and Poet.* The latter volume deals with Muir's
life from the point of view of an interested scholar. Butter principally fills
in areas that the poet only sketched—as, for instance, in the first chapter,
where details about Muir's birthplace Orkney and the particulars of Muir's
early environment are examined. Speaking of Muir's family background in
the country, Butter points out that

> they gave Muir a childhood in which he could see his vision of
> Eden, but also perhaps contributed, though blamelessly, to his
> difficulties and inner divisions in the Glasgow years, and to his
> lateness in finding his true vocation as a poet.[35]

Perhaps more central to Muir is the fact that in his early youth he had in
Orkney

> a landscape which combines many things in a harmonious way—
> the human present and the past; the life of men, of animals and
> of the earth; land, sea, and sky.[36]

33. Ibid., p. 22.

34. Peter Butter, *Edwin Muir* (New York: Grove, 1962).

35. Peter Butter, *Edwin Muir: Man and Poet*, p. 3.

36. Ibid., p. 6

As is often the case, the series of experiences with farms or the country in youth had their part in producing a certain quality of common sense, an adequate vision with respect to what is most noteworthy in life, an abiding distaste for cant and bullying, and a steadfast unwillingness to move away from important vital centers of experience.

If any poem is indicative of Muir's own feeling for his youth, it is "Childhood:"

Childhood

Long time he lay upon the sunny hill,
　　To his father's house below securely bound.
Far off the silent, changing sound was still,
　　With the black islands laying thick around.

He saw each separate height, each vaguer hue,
　　Where the massed islands rolled in mist away,
And though all ran together in his view
　　He knew that unseen straits between them lay.

Often he wondered what new shores were there.
　　In thought he saw the still light on the sand,
The shallow water clear in tranquil air,
　　And walked through it in joy from strand to strand.

Over the sound a ship so slow would pass
　　That in the black hill's gloom it seemed to lie.
The evening sound was smooth like sunken glass,
　　And time seemed finished ere the ship passed by.

Grey tiny rocks slept round him where he lay,
　　Moveless as they, more still as evening came,
The grasses threw straight shadows far away,
　　And from the house his mother called his name.[37]

It is hardly insignificant that the father is mentioned in connection with the home in the somewhat extended sense of the father being a holder of property, a provider, or a protective agent, or that the mother's place in this poem is that of a maternal being, a dutiful helper, and also a protective safeguard. To stretching the point, the suggestion is that Muir was grateful

37. "Childhood," p. 19.

for what family life he was able to enjoy. As central to an appreciation of
the whole poem is the awareness of "identity in solitude": that past time
when an individual in his youth considered his relation to the scheme of
things in a meditative spirit (a familiar experience for young people or
children, and a familiar and present memory for an older person).

What is not often stressed by scholars of Muir is the toughness and
cosmopolitan skill he acquired in dealing with an urban environment during
the hard years in Glasgow, before he was able to be a professional man of
letters:

> His contemporaries were rough, realistic, Rabelaisian—
> hide-bound intellectually, but in their actual contact with life less
> puritanical than he was. After the initial shocks he was able to
> make friends. He was getting over his priggish religiosity and
> adapting himself to ordinary people, but his deeper self was in
> abeyance.[38]

Whether in London, Rome, Prague, or Edinburgh, Muir gravitated naturally
toward the central figures in existing artistic society. His good judgment
is perhaps explained by the experiences in Glasgow, where he achieved a
better perspective on how to act with respect to life experience than most
people are capable of. Also, the earlier tastes of reality in the Scottish
seaport created the means to life that help explain why Muir (living in
urban centers most of his adult life) remained consistently a great artist
under conditions that would have silenced many writers or driven them
toward a sentimental escapism. The early urban environment helped Muir
to adjust to the harshness of city existence without a slackening off of the
artistic powers. It was at the age of fifty, in 1937, that he was able to
publish *Journeys and Places*.[39] At the age of fifty-six came *The Narrow
Place*,[40] at fifty-nine *The Voyage and Other Poems*,[41] at sixty-two *The
Labyrinth*,[42] and at sixty-nine *One Foot in Eden*[43]—all among his most
outstanding works.

38. Butter, *Edwin Muir: Man and Poet*, p. 30.

39. *Journeys and Places* (London: Dent, 1937).

40. *The Narrow Place* (London: Faber, 1943).

41. *The Voyage and Other Poems* (London: Faber, 1946).

42. *The Labyrinth* (London: Faber, 1949).

43. *One Foot in Eden* (London: Faber, 1956).

II

Muir, The German Tradition, and Metaphysics

It is not inappropriate, at this point, to speak again of Franz Kafka and Edwin Muir together, for many of Muir's attitudes and experiences with respect to the great novelist can form a prelude to the discussion of the Scotsman's poems. Both men can be seen in relation to nightmares, and many works of the Czech who wrote in German reflect a complete spiritual disenchantment with reality. In fact, Kafka produced more accurate depictions of the modern religious malaise than any earlier writer or artist. Before Kafka, nihilism had often been depicted—as in Macbeth's cries of despair—as the result of special or unusual situations. At the time that Kafka wrote, nihilism and pessimism were ways of life founded on psychological and metaphysical reality, an attitude that affected his English translator, Edwin Muir, who filled in the religious void created by Kafka with poetic structures reasserting the value and worth of traditional human experiences —experiences such as appreciation of other people, love, contribution to general and individual human happiness, salvation, spiritual richness, emotional plenty, and economic wealth.

A story like "The Transformation,"[1] which Willa and Edwin Muir translated (or what is called "The Metamorphosis" in the American edition of *In the Penal Settlement: Tales and Short Pieces*),[2] produced in most readers a kind of fascinated but rebellious nausea with respect to what can happen to a person in a world where the unexpected is commonplace. Gregor Samsa is a kind of complete victim:

> As Gregor Samsa awoke one morning from uneasy dreams he found himself transformed in his bed into a gigantic insect.[3]

1. Franz Kafka, *In the Penal Settlement*, tr. Edwin and Willa Muir (London: Secker, 1949), pp. 63–128.

2. Franz Kafka, *The Penal Colony*, tr. Edwin and Willa Muir (New York: Schocken, 1959), pp. 67–132.

3. Kafka, *In the Penal Settlement*, p. 63

One is reminded upon further consideration that most of the heroes in Kafka's work start and end up as victims of one thing or another. Indeed, as "The Transformation" unveils itself to the reader, the modern Gothic spirit achieves one of its most horrific and yet ridiculous triumphs. Such an unattractive portrait and ending for a story can produce in the careful reader or translator the desire to create a new type of character—particularly the reader concerned with the creation of exemplary personae to be imitated by audiences. In other words, a vacuum has been created in the area of what one might call significant or worthy personae.

Love is another topic that Kafka examined carefully. In a book like *The Trial* relationships are used to heighten the dilemmas that the hero feels and experiences: it is at the beginning of the hero's downfall that Fräulein Bürstner comes into his life in a meaningful sense. This is not something that is explained by Kafka; rather, there is a kind of ambiguous quality about the timing. One is not sure if Fräulein Bürstner is interested in K. because she sympathizes with him and his plight, or if she is perversely drawn to the dramatics inherent in K.'s situation—the fact that he is soon to die terribly. Also, there is a faint suggestion that she is a prostitute. Perhaps even more sinister is the implicit suggestion that Fräulein Bürstner is somehow or other involved in the cause-and-effect relationships leading to the execution scene:

> And then before them Fräulein Bürstner appeared, mounting a small flight of steps leading into the square from a low-lying side-street. It was not quite certain that it was she, but the resemblance was close enough. Whether it were really Fräulein Bürstner or not, however, did not matter to K.; the important thing was that he suddenly realized the futility of resistance.[4]

At the beginning of the next paragraph:

> Fräulein Bürstner meanwhile had gone round the bend into a side-street, but by this time K. could do without her and submitted himself to the guidance of his escort. In complete harmony all three now made their way across a bridge in the moonlight, the two men readily yielded to K.'s slightest movement, and when he turned slightly towards the parapet they turned, too, in a solid front.[5]

4. Franz Kafka, *The Trial*, tr. Edwin and Willa Muir (London: Secker, 1968), p. 251.

5. Ibid., p. 252.

There are few passages so tragically and terribly oriented which deal with the question of the nature of feminine control of men. It cannot be proved (as far as I know) that there is a reaction on the part of Muir, to speak in terms of Arnold Toynbee's formula, to the dark, murky visions of Franz Kafka. Nevertheless, one cannot help feeling that Muir as an ambitious artist perhaps would be interested in providing a sharply contrasting, alternative vision—one that could operate either consciously or unconsciously. At any rate he must have felt challenged. I will suggest that the love poetry of Edwin Muir sharply, and rather unsentimentally, contrasts with the work of Kafka, particularly insofar as certain values are posited and deeply explored as being good and worthwhile in themselves.

In addition to depicting human beings and lovers in a reduced situation, Kafka was also aware of another related problem. Muir put it this way:

> The frustration of the hero is an intrinsic part of Kafka's theme; and it is caused by what in theological language is known as the irreconcilability of the divine and the human law; a subtle yet immeasurable disparity. Out of this dilemma Kafka fashions his stories, or rather his story, for it is one story; he has nothing else to tell.[6]

Indeed, the disparity between human hopes and what one might call divine law—the way things work out for people—is apparent to any sensible observer. Kafka expressed this in abbreviated form in this part of the parable "Before the Law," which Muir and his wife translated and which is also a section of *The Trial:*

> Before the Law stands a doorkeeper on guard. To this doorkeeper there comes a man from the country who begs for admittance to the Law. But the doorkeeper says that he cannot admit the man at the moment. The man, on reflection, asks if he will be allowed, then, to enter later. 'It is possible;' answers the doorkeeper, 'but not at this moment.' Since the door leading into the Law stands open as usual and 'the doorkeeper steps to one side, the man bends down to peer through the entrance. When the doorkeeper sees that, he laughs and says: 'If you are so strongly tempted, try to get in without my permission. But note that I am powerful. And I am only the lowest doorkeeper. From hall to hall keepers stand at every door, one more powerful than the

6. *Essays on Literature and Society* (Boston: Harvard University Press, 1965), p. 122.

other. Even the third of these has an aspect that even I cannot
bear to look at.' These are difficulties which the man from the
country has not expected to meet, the Law, he thinks, should be
accessible to every man and at all times, but when he looks more
closely at the doorkeeper in his furred robe, with his huge point-
ed nose and long, thin, Tartar beard, he decides that he had better wait until he gets permission to enter.[7]

This passage suggests the unattainability of divine law. *The Trial* itself, as a
whole, goes beyond the problem of never knowing the truth, and suggests
through its unhappy conclusion that reality is in itself malicious, vicious,
forboding, evil, and dangerous. Such conceptions—both the disparity between the real and the ideal, and the actual evil nature of life—are far short
of what a person might hope to find in existence. Indeed, as I shall suggest
later, the poetry of Edwin Muir proceeds from these disintegrations of
metaphysical hopes to find data in the course of experience that is valuable
in itself. This comes out particularly in the place poems, which involve
metaphysical explorations of imaginative "regions."

Muir, finally, touches on one more problem in his criticism of Kafka
while discussing the problem of "vocation...one's true place," and of "acting in accordance with the will of heavenly powers":

The problem with which all Kafka's work is concerned is a
moral and spiritual one. It is a twofold problem: that of *finding
one's true vocation, one's true place, whatever it may be, in
the community*; and that of *acting in accordance with the will
of heavenly powers*. But though it has those two aspects it was
in his eyes a single problem; for a man's true place in the community is finally determined not by secular, but by divine, law,
and only when, by apparent chance or deliberate effort, a man
finds himself in his divinely appointed place, can he live as he
should. Many people slip into their place without being aware of
it; others are painfully conscious of the difficulty, the evident
impossibility, of finding any place at all; and nobody has been
more clearly and deeply conscious of it, I think, than Kafka. Two
things no doubt exacerbated his feeling of being shut out from
the community: that he was of Jewish blood, and that he was an
invalid, and thus doubly isolated. Yet it would be trivial to attach
first importance to these things, which did not give rise to the

7. Franz Kafka, *Parables*, tr. Edwin and Willa Muir (New York: Schocken, 1937). p. 45.

problem, but merely accentuated it. For the problem is an eternal one, eternal, that is, failing the realisation of a perfect society, which is inconceivable. It is also a problem that has become crucial in our time, where we see tradition after tradition crumbling, and society itself a chaos in which it is hard to find one's way, far less a vocation that has a transcendent sanction. The greatness of Kafka lies not in his having solved the problem, which would be absurd, but rather in his having realised it as it has never been realised before, illuminating it with a power of imagination and thought unexampled in his time.

Roughly this seems to me to be the theme of all Kafka's work, a theme in which is involved the *mystery of divine law and the mystery of human life*, both of which it touches simultaneously. The full originality of his imagination, the opulence of his invention, the reader may be left to enjoy by himself.[8]

I suggest that these concerns with finding an imaginative "place" or myth for modern man (evident in the phrases italicized in this quotation) became those of Muir in his last years as a writer. He was involved with the business of finding an adequate savior figure—or at least building one that took account of the nature of life on earth adequately. He attempted to go beyond the quality of the seeker Kafka's *The Castle*[9] in his dramatic depictions, and he often succeeded.

If one takes the time and trouble to read through the list of complete and published translations by Willa and Edwin Muir,[10] one can see that many writers besides Franz Kafka had much to do with the poet's development as an artist and thinker. Gerhart Hauptmann, Lion Feuchtwanger, Ludwig Renn, Ernst Glaeser, Emil Alphons Rheinhardt, Kurt Heuser, Hermann Broch, Ernst Lothar, Shalom Asch, Heinrich Mann, Erik Maria von Kühnelt-Leddihn, Robert Neumann, Georges Maurice Pale'ologue, Carl Jakob Burckhardt, and Zsolt Harsányi all can be seen as playing important roles in the growth and development of the Scotsman. Indeed, in the same sense that T. S. Eliot reacted to the optimism of the Victorians or was technically influenced by his Symbolist forebearers, or Ezra Pound incorporated the spirit

8. Introduction to Franz Kafka, *Description of a Struggle and the Great Wall of China* (London: Secker, 1960), pp. 14–15. Emphasis added.

9. Franz Kafka, *The Castle*, tr. Edwin and Willa Muir (London: Secker, 1965).

10. Elgin Mellown, *Bibliography of the Writings of Edwin Muir* (London: Vane, 1966), pp. 121–125.

of much of classical poetry of the East and West in his work, or W. H.
Auden's thought stemmed out of a profound consideration of Marxist-
Leninist doctrines, one can see Edwin Muir growing as a poet from his
experiences translating many of the important German and central European novels of the early part of this century. The fictional world of many
of these books is as strange, tormented, and torn as was the historical
reality of the time. Perhaps the fact that Muir did not have a normal university education meant that his reviews, readings, and translations dealing
with foreign cultures had a more powerful effect on him than is usual. With
other writers the influences from without were more likely to have been a
commonly shared and uniform English tradition, the classics, or just the
masterworks of one or two foreign, modern national literatures—those
works taught in certain ways at the universities in Great Britain.

For instance, Ludwig Renn's *War* could be seen as directly related to
poems like "The Combat,"[11] "The Little General,"[12] "Then,"[13] and "Troy."[14]
In theme one can see *After War* in connection with poems like "The Refugees,"[15] "Scotland 1941,"[16] or "After a Hypothetical War,"[17] or in terms of
realistic narrative technique, as related to *An Autobiography*[18] or *The Story
and the Fable*.[19] *The Life of Eleonora Duse* presented a great woman in
some detail; the complimentary or realistic depiction of women crops up in
Muir's poetry in poems like "For Ann Scott-Moncrieff (1914-1943),"[20]
"Penelope in Doubt,"[21] "The Two Sisters,"[22] and "An Island Tale."[23] Stylis-

11. "The Combat," pp. 179-180.

12. "The Little General," pp. 110-111.

13. "Then," pp. 94-95.

14. "Troy," p. 71.

15. "The Refugees," pp. 95-96.

16. "Scotland 1941," pp. 97-98.

17. "After a Hypothetical War," p. 265.

18. *An Autobiography* (London: Methuen, 1968).

19. *The Story and the Fable* (London: Harrap, 1940).

20. "For Ann Scott-Moncrieff (1914-1943)," pp. 156-157.

21. "Penelope in Doubt," p. 277.

22. "The Two Sisters," pp. 281-282.

23. "An Island Tale," pp. 266-267.

tically, Muir's poetry can be seen as having taken on a certain aesthetic edge right at about the time he was working on Burckhardt's *Richelieu;* perhaps Burckhardt's language forced Muir into a poetic style that was baroque, dense, sure, brilliant, and well ordered. *Mottke the Thief* and the *Hill of Lies* take on the color of much of Muir's descriptive work in connection with his early, unpleasant experiences in industrialized Glasgow. Muir's early translation of Hauptmann's *Veland* seems somehow related to his later poem "Sick Caliban";[24] Hauptmann's *Indipohdi* to Muir's later grapplings with a Christ or antichrist figure; *A Winter Ballad* could be seen as creating a psychological experience that later produced poems like "The Difficult Land,"[25] or lines like

> Yet here there is no word, no sign
> But quiet murder in the street.[26]

The historical tone of Feuchtwanger's *Josephus* or *The Jew of Rome* is not unlike the historically oriented *One Foot in Eden,*[27] Muir's last published book of poetry. In all cases, the influences seem foreign to the experiences of his immediate contemporaries.

The mass of interrelations between Muir's translations and Muir's own writings is endless in its details; yet the point of view from which I feel Muir can most adequately be seen as a poet of genuine value for the latter part of the twentieth century is more in terms of his attitudes toward religion and myth. His experience with Franz Kafka and with the other writers I have mentioned has to do with metaphysics and a separate, individual, different way of looking at life. Kafka can be thought of as "sweeping everyday reality under the table"; but it is rather the metaphysical emptiness (or viciousness) of his world that turned Muir's attention toward the modern predicament and modern man's need for salvation.

Writing in the *New Republic* in 1941, he contrasted the modern novel with that of Fielding and Jane Austen:

> All I mean is that they lived in an order in which everybody possessed without thinking about it very much the feeling for a permanence above earthly permanence; in which they believed that the ceaseless flux of human existence passed against an un-

24. "Sick Caliban," pp. 276–277.

25. "The Difficult Land," pp. 237–238.

26. "The Town Betrayed," pp. 76–77.

27. *One Foot in Eden* (London: Faber, 1956).

changeable background ruled by immutable values which they
called God or Eternity or the Absolute. They felt—they did not
merely believe—that there was a relation between the short existence of man and that unchangeable world; and this sentiment,
in whatever terms it was expressed, was the final earnest of the
completeness of their conception of life, showing that it em-
braced everything, God and man, eternity and time, the universe
and humanity.[28]

Our own situation in this century is different:

Is there any universal mark by which we can recognize a conception of human life that is complete, all-embracing and in a
high sense normal to mankind?[29]

In a very harsh and dangerous century, the answer to this question is
obviously no for many modern men. Yet one must look somewhere for significance in life:

But the norm of human existence remains. There are certain
conceptions and beliefs that are natural to man, that satisfy his
mind and heart better than any alternative ones, and without
which he cannot live for long. The mark of such conceptions is
their completeness: they close the circle. In a state of irremedi-
able imperfection, such as man's, the circle can be closed only by
calling on something beyond man: by postulating a transcen-
dental reality. So the belief in eternity is natural to man. And all
the arts, all the forms of literature, since they depend on that
belief, are equally natural to man. When that belief partially fails,
imagination suffers an eclipse, and art becomes a problem instead
of a function. If that belief were to fail completely and for good,
it is possible that it would mean the end of all imaginative literature and art. But it is inconceivable that it should fail, for it is
native to man.[30]

The "certain conceptions and beliefs that are natural to man" are what Muir
is chiefly concerned about in his poetry. The broken world of central
Europe presented in many respects some of the worst tragedies of modern

28. "The Status of the Novel," *New Republic* 105 (11 August 1941), p. 194.

29. Ibid.

30. Ibid., pp. 194–195.

European life, tragedies whose horror Kafka was to reflect in his novels; and from the fragments of this broken civilization, Muir went on to create a body of language that serves some of the needs of myth and by its very nature pays tribute to the sacred. If one can speak of Kafka as presenting the most extreme types of psychological nightmares, then one can speak of Muir as providing, often, just the opposite. With Muir one has the ever-present sense of nightmare, but the structure of that nightmare in Muir takes on new forms, or else is buried. Often, however, something else valuable in itself shows above ground, much in the way that Kafka's *Amerika* followed *The Trial* and *The Castle*, but more frequently the best poetry of Muir; that is, the phenomenon of language transcending itself with the worth of referential significance and actuality. One feels more often in Muir than in Kafka that metaphor lends itself to good actions—to discovering meaning in life and acting upon it. By taking the imagery, content, and interpretations of Edwin Muir's poetry for what they are, we are best able to relate to the earlier nightmare world that Muir was drawn to (the world reflected by Kafka and other central European novelists of the first third of the century), and at the same time move forward with something in mind that creates in great detail values for modern man. It is not accidental that there are many who take modern poetry more seriously than the sacraments of formal religion; Muir, in a spirit of disequilibrium with the forms of life that the twentieth century often took—a disequilibrium shared by other modern poets such as Rilke in the *Duino Elegies* or T. S. Eliot in the *Four Quartets*—worked in language that could provide material for a new religion. Through seeing a part of Muir's accomplishment as a man of letters, we shall often be able to see how Muir relates to and creates proper attitudes toward possible ultimate truths or universals; and we shall see how his poetic patterns can help men and women to live more adequately, prosperously, happily, and usefully in the context of the contemporary world.

III

Despair

Human love (both intellectual and sensuous) between the two sexes, a perennial topic in Muir's poems, receives perhaps its most problematical and tragic treatment in four of his earliest and best poems—"Betrayal,"[1] "The Enchanted Knight,"[2] "Tristram's Journey,"[3] and "Hölderlin's Journey."[4] Love was to be one of the recurring themes in a great number of Muir's poems, as he built up the body of his most worthy and most significant writings—the work he wished to preserve. Finally, in the *Collected Poems* of 1965,[5] one can find as many as fifty or sixty verse artifacts built and structured with romantic and heterosexual love experience as the sole subject matter; or as possible interpretation of a poem; or as a dominant, characteristic, or very noticeable theme. One might take as the starting point for the discussion the medium-sized sentence in "Autumn in Prague,"[6] with its effective proliferation and repetitions of short and then long *e* sounds in the final words of each line break in the middle of the poem:

> In the meadow the goat-herd,
> A young girl,
> Sits with bent head,
> Blind, covered head,
> Bowed to the earth,

1. "Betrayal," p. 21.

2. "The Enchanted Knight," p. 74.

3. "Tristram's Journey," pp. 64–66.

4. "Hölderlin's Journey," pp. 66–68.

5. *Collected Poems* (New York: Oxford University Press, 1965).

6. "Autumn in Prague," p. 23.

Like a tree
Dreaming a long-held dream.

This is the starting point for male love: the young girl. In the same poem
the earlier statement

All meanings have fallen into your lap,
Uncomprehending earth.

serves to increase our growing sense of importance and worthiness with
respect to this pastoral scene. Indeed, the poem works toward

the peace, the exhaustion, the sense of energy withdrawn but
still existing in suspense, the coldness and clarity, the sense of
having been unburdened and of bareness—these are all features
at once of the landscape and of the poet's state.[7]

The pastoral territory with the "girl" (more appropriate in the modern
world than a "shepherdess") not only conveys the sense of an action as
having possibly passed by, but also seems more explicitly expressive of
potentiality or latency with respect to what the situation might offer in
terms of development, evolution, and movement. It is indeed the case that
Muir (himself but recently married at the time "Autumn in Prague" was
written) was exploring a new situation and looking at it with fresh eyes. A
reconciling tone and mature reflective wisdom prevail in the poem's tone
and quality. But just as important as that is this picture of the adolescent
turned from frivolous girlhood to a striking, perhaps apprehensive, and
moving figure in a perennial and recurrent landscape. The scene coordinates
with a sensitively drawn, hypothetical archetype of a young girl in anticipation, as a product of nature, or of a young woman in readiness. The
drama comes in connection with the relatively detached emotions of the
quiet narrative voice of the poem in relationship to "the girl in nature."
These descriptions of the goatherd, taken in connection with the entire
corpus of the poetry, serve as an effective prelude to the tragic tone of the
early love poems, in the sense that we begin an examination of two poetic
personae—the author and she who may be a present, past, or future lover,
or never a lover. The sense of calm and quiet latency and potentiality is
very central in this particular case. Also as important and refreshing is the
relative absence of artifice and ceremony—the absence of implements of

---

7. Peter Butter, *Edwin Muir: Man and Poet* (Edinburgh: Oliver, 1966), p. 99.

wantonness and lust. Perhaps the poet had some of the simple love lyrics of Heine in mind.

It has been said that Edwin Muir's poetry often has a rather obscure or tenuous logic; but if one keeps in mind that that poetry is often concerned with expressing imaginative states of consciousness—making visions or dreams—then many of the poems assume a high degree of logical and rational realism. Although it is often helpful to assume a logic appropriate to the occasion, the poems can convey themselves clearly without outside help. Such a poem is "Betrayal," which presents a scene that can only be described, like the terrain of Coleridge's "Ancient Mariner," as an imaginative, phantasmal landscape. The poem deals with an enduring problem:

Betrayal

Sometimes I see, caught in a snare,
　One with a foolish lovely face,
Who stands with scattered moon-struck air
　Alone, in a wild woody place.

She was entrapped there long ago.
　Yet fowler none has come to see
His prize; though all the tree-trunks show
　A front of silent treachery.

And there she waits, while in her flesh
　Small joyless teeth fret without rest.
But she stands smiling in the mesh,
　While she is duped and dispossest.

I know her name; for it is told
　That beauty is a prisoner,
And that her gaoler, bleak and bold,
　Scores her fine flesh, and murders her.

He slays her with invisible hands,
　And inly wastes her flesh away,
And strangles her with stealthy bands;
　Melts her as snow day after day.

Within his thicket life decays
　And slow is changed by hidden guile;
And nothing now of Beauty stays,
　Save her divine and witless smile.

> For still she smiles, and does not know
> Her feet are in the snaring lime.
> He who entrapped her long ago.
> And kills her, is unpitying Time.

A statement made after Muir's death by T. S. Eliot, as he considered the 1965 grouping of the poems, is perhaps most appropriate:

> But when I came to study the volume of his *Collected Poems*, before publication, I was struck, as I had not been before, by the power of his early work.[8]

"Betrayal" is such an earlier poem, and it is appropriate that we keep in mind the familiar lines of Andrew Marvell in "To His Coy Mistress":

> Had we but World enough, and Time,
> This coyness, Lady, were no crime.

and

> But at my back I alwaies hear
> Times winged Charriot hurrying near:

Marvell is at once playful, humorous, and serious in his treatment of time and beauty; the sense we have with Muir is that of very high seriousness, terror, nightmare, and a concern with altering a problem through recognizing and explaining it. Part of the drama involves the fact that the poet-narrator must have suffered, like most of us, from these problems.

In the fourth stanza Muir leaves the poem open to two possible interpretations. If the female protagonist is semihuman, then we are dealing with a human situation between two people. If we take "beauty" as a goddess, and "Time" as a god, we are able to look at the poem in mythological, as well as historical, terms. By means of this deliberate or accidental ambiguity, Muir deals with his theme of the destruction of feminine grace on both a human and a metaphysical level at the same time. The terms of "capture" reverse the story of Venus and Adonis. If we think of the fate of Puccini's principal feminine character in *Madam Butterfly*, Cio-Cio-San. we are reminded of something beyond the mere devastation of beauty by time: the relationship of that devastation to male treachery. The poem, however, achieves a high enough degree of pathos through its exploration

8. T. S. Eliot in Muir, *Collected Poems*, p. 4.

of the theme of beauty and time. We learn the girl is "caught in a snare," is "duped and dispossest." Her captor "bleak and bold/Scores her fine flesh, and murders her." She has a "scattered moon-struck air," and she is being strangled slowly. The evil agent "inly wastes her flesh away" as well as "Melts her as snow day after day." Most significantly,

> nothing now of beauty stays,
> Save her divine and witless smile

Not only is Time opposed to her beauty, but perhaps even more importantly, time as in its manifestations as "civilization" could be suggested by "her gaoler" if we wished to extend our interpretation. One has the continual feeling of a destructive and pathetic torpor as the poem evolves in its terrible and unrelenting logic. The work serves as a warning to those of great physical and intellectual beauty who are intent on the past, as distinct from those who are concerned with evolving and growing toward new and more significant experiences—those involved with morally active decisions or otherwise. Indeed, the question at the end of "Merlin"[9] becomes even more relevant in light of this issue:

> Will your magic ever show
> The sleeping bride shut in her bower,
> The day wreathed in its mound of snow
> And Time locked in his tower?

Perhaps a poem more true to what is really the situation in life is "The Enchanted Knight" (another poem with a setting that is medieval and contains material that is similar to our ideas of courtly love). Here the dilemma is reversed: the protagonist is male:

The Enchanted Knight

> Lulled by La Belle Dame Sans Merci he lies
>   In the bare wood below the blackening hill.
> The plough drives nearer now, the shadow flies
>   Past him across the plain, but he lies still.
>
> Long since the rust its gardens here has planned,
>   Flowering his armour like an autumn field.

---

9. "Merlin," pp. 73–74.

From his sharp breast-plate to his iron hand
  A spider's web is stretched, a phantom shield.

When footsteps pound the turf beside his ear
  Armies pass through his dream in endless line,
And one by one his ancient friends appear;
  They pass all day, but he can make no sign.

When a bird cries within the silent grove
  The long-lost voice goes by, he makes to rise
And follow, but his cold limbs never move,
  And on the turf unstirred his shadow lies.

But if a withered leaf should drift
  Across his face and rest, the dread drops start
Chill on his forehead. Now he tries to lift
  The insulting weight that stays and breaks his heart.

The early poems of Edwin Muir are characterized by a fascination with the quatrain (a form that also interested John Crowe Ransom, as well as many Europeans); the poet was to find newer or looser structures for his ideas as time went on. Also, his language was to become less general in quality, more in line with Imagistic ideas about choice of diction. In "The Enchanted Knight," various pronunciations of *i* seem characteristic, and it is probably not accidental that "I" should figure in a poem about the self or ego. The use of *i* and the consistent rhyme scheme seem to underline the monotonous bewilderment and frustration of the figure described in the poem. In this work, in fact, there is more perhaps that is symbolic and suggestive than one can find in the works of those called Symbolist poets. The "range of indication" extends, as P. H. Butter[10] notes, far beyond the literal and matter-of-fact sense: some of the themes suggested by Butter include the importance of the "psychological place" (Butter is no doubt thinking of the theme of bewilderment in love), death in life, neuroses, or La Belle Dame as equivalent to the Muse in her soporific role. In Keats's poem "La Belle Dame sans Merci" the emphasis is on the value of memory or a dream-like state of with respect to recapturing the sensual essence of a situation; romantic love is the predominant value. In the case of Muir, it is a belief in the fatal destructiveness of love that is stressed, more than it is in Keats. Images such as "lulled," "blackening hill," "he can make no sign," "dread

10. Peter Butter, *Edwin Muir* (New York: Grove, 1962), pp. 62–64.

drops start/Chill on his forehead," and "insulting weight" reinforce this interpretation. P. H. Butter's comment is appropriate and apt:

> He is alienated from the world of action, but is still in some way aware of it. Something like this is quite common in dreams. One has a despairing sense of helplessness and immobility, while knowing that some action is urgently necessary; one's limbs or one's tongue will not obey one; the feeling is similar to that conveyed by the last stanza of the poem.[11]

As important as interpretating the poem this way might be pondering it as a kind of archetypal instance of schizophrenia in love—either in the recognition that pain, and therefore hallucination, and subsequently a lack of action accompany romantic experience, or, with respect to a total involvement, the horrible and helpless sense that one is not able to do anything about the destruction or ebbing away of what was once a profound commitment. Helplessness in love is the key concept to the understanding of this poem—and the poem's centralness and universality are increased by the fact that a large percentage of people, particularly young men, undergo a very highly charged, horrible experience with a romantic love object.

Two other early poems play upon related themes. In "Tristram's Journey," a human reaction to and confrontation with the dramatic evil of a particular situation receives scrutiny. A kind of reconciliation (perhaps one should speak of fate in this case) is brought about by the poet as he sees the scene where as Tristram looked at his lover:

> The round walls hardened as he looked,
> And he was in his place.

In this case as in most, reading the whole poem is helpful in moving toward the center of interpretation:

Tristram's Journey

> He strode across the room and flung
>   The letter down: 'You need not tell
> Your treachery, harlot!' He was gone
>   Ere Iseult fainting fell.
>
> He rode out from Tintagel gate,
>   He heard his charger slowly pace,

---

11. Ibid., p. 63.

And ever hung a cloud of gnats
  Three feet before his face.

At a wood's border he turned round
  And saw the distant castle side,
Iseult looking towards the wood,
  Mark's window gaping wide.

He turned again and slowly rode
  Into the forest's flickering shade,
And now as sunk in waters green
  Were armour, helm, and blade.

First he awoke with night around
  And heard the wind, and woke again
At noon within a ring of hills,
  At sunset on a plain.

And hill and plain and wood and tower
  Passed on and on and turning came
Back to him, tower and wood and hill,
  Now different, now the same.

There was a castle on a lake.
  The castle doubled in the mere
Confused him, his uncertain eye
  Wavered from there to here.

A window in the wall had held
  Iseult upon a summer day,
While he and Polomide below
  Circled in furious fray.

But now he searched the towers, the sward,
  And struggled something to recall,
A stone, a shadow. Blank the lake,
  And empty every wall.

He left his horse, left sword and mail,
  And went into the woods and tore
The branches from the clashing trees
  Until his rage was o'er.

And now he wandered on the hills
  In peace. Among the shepherd's flocks

Often he lay so long, he seemed
   One of the rocks.

The shepherds called and made him run
   Like a tame cur to round the sheep.
At night he lay among the dogs
   Beside a well to sleep.

And he forgot Iseult and all.
   Dagonet once and two came by
Like tall escutcheoned animals
   With antlers towering high.

He snapped their spears, rove off their helms,
   And beat them with his hands and sent
Them onward with a bitter heart,
   But knew not where they went.

They came to Mark and told him how
   A madman ruled the hinds and kept
The wandering sheep. Mark haled him to
   Tintagel while he slept.

He woke and saw King Mark at chess
   And Iseult with her maids at play,
The arras where the scarlet knights
   And ladies stood all day.

None knew him. In the garden once
   Iseult walked in the afternoon,
Her hound leapt up and licked his face,
   Iseult fell in a swoon.

There as he leaned the misted grass
   Cleared blade by blade below his face,
The round walls hardened as he looked,
   And he was in his place.

In reading Muir's "Tristram's Journey" we can, of course, be aware of
Gottfried von Strassburg, and can think of ourselves as dealing with a
character from epic literature. Indeed, Muir, through his choice of Tristram
as a persona, bolsters the lore around this figure. By working in what many
contemporary critics would call the realm of the intellectual poem, the poet

proceeds with a common and shared artistic story—a story for the intelligentsia. There is glory in the figure of Tristram in the Gottfried version, and there is tragic suffering involved in the dilemma of the chief protagonists; yet the Muir version attains a certain significant rapport of its own with the reader. This is particularly true if we think of "Tristram's Journey" as both a continuation and an ending for the older, better-known version— that reading matter of kings that contrasts so sharply with the Muir poem. The reduction of the great character to rubble, and the preliminary sorrow with respect to final loss upon separation from his Iseult, are what is so terrifying if we keep in mind Gottfried's account. If anything it is the appeal of pity that makes Muir's poem move to its almost predetermined conclusion; it might be said that the poet-savior forgives our sin and puts history back in its correct place. To use the terminology of Albert Camus, a terrible absurdity is replaced by one that is even more fraught with terror. The moral lesson against adultery of Gottfried's epic receives, in a way, a reinforcement, for in the Muir version the terror and nightmarish aspects of the situation increase through the horrid reduction of Tristram to complete personal chaos, total disorder, and anarchical disenchantment.

After surveying "Tristram's Journey," we note in the first stanza that the ballad manners and numbers of the poet surprise us even more than they would in the conventional story situation. We feel surprised at Mark's even more diminished role in the triangle. He is a logical choice for attention in what might be described as a theoretical Tristram variation—one concerned with the less happy details of the legend. By dealing with a "crucial episode,"[12] a fragment of a story, the lyric poet, the master of the short poem, sufficiently satisfies our sense of the ballad form. By establishing a narrative line more saturated with "happenings" as distinct from intellectual exploration, and by the submergence of the self to a relatively detached observer and overseer of the events, the ballad maker conveys his experience of a segment of the Tristram legend. Perhaps it is more significant to speak of a sub-archetypal figure: the adulterer-lover as tragic figure and pawn. This is in itself to speak in terms of a reduction of Tristram in the Gottfried version; however, Muir's poem seems to carry no such reduction in its essential and characteristic terms.

Our sense of moral credulity may flounder slightly at the tragic quality

12. Alex Preminger, *Encyclopedia of Poetry and Poetics* (Princeton: Princeton University Press, 1965), p. 62.

of the indisputable moral dilemma involved in the love triangle of Mark, Tristram, and Iseult (and perhaps even another lover, making the figure a rectangle). In reading the Muir version as if in answer to a hope for the poem somehow easing our own tragic burden, as well as the protagonist's, our moral sympathy for the characters "happens," and our reconciliation to the situation occurs as the poem assumes its finest imaginative demarcation. This episode involves the reaction of the shepherds to Tristram's forceable eviction of the dagonets. As if in appreciation for his useful act, and perhaps more in sympathy with the range and subtle introspection that surrounds the laceration of the beasts, the shepherds move toward reconciling Tristram with his destiny, not necessarily knowing this may be a tragic fate, a kind of predetermined farce.

In a particular sense, "persona control" in spite of the theme of evil in love is an important device in the poem. One feels that if Muir were asked to point a moral for the versework, "Tristram's Journey," he might respond by saying that in this particular poem life and love are evil; but through the agency of common sense, through the "denouncement of recognition" by Tristram of his own place, and through the inconclusive feeling of suspense with which the poem ends, we achieve through the recognition of the ideals of reason and common sense moral compatibility and reconciliation. We see that a fate such as Tristram's may include a partial resolution of the conflict and therefore attain a partial purgation of our own worst tendencies. The poem, in a final sense, is about idealism, and the necessity for idealism to deal adequately with the true nature of things—particularly insofar as idealism in love is able to initiate positive change. One is left with a sense of security; or, as the street-corner philosopher might put it, we are left in love most basically and ultimately with a concern for "bread and butter." And finally, it is the shepherds, in a way, who are the worse blasphemers of moral law:

> The shepherds called and made him run
> Like a tame cur to round the sheep.

Perhaps their force initiated hope in Tristram for a less brutal process for change in this particular human love affair.

It is of course no accident that Muir picked a love story about Hölderlin, the German poet who was so tragic a lover in his real life, as a significant theme for a poem:

Hölderlin's Journey

When Hölderlin started from Bordeaux
    He was not mad but lost in mind,
For time and space had fled away
    With her he had to find.

'The morning bells rang over France
    From tower to tower. At noon I came
Into a maze of little hills,
    Head-high and every hill the same.

'A little world of emerald hills,
    And at their heart a faint bell tolled;
Wedding or burial, who could say?
    For death, unseen, is bold.

'Too small to climb, too tall to show
    More than themselves, the hills lay round.
Nearer to her, or farther? They
    Might have stretched to the world's bound.

'A shallow candour was their all,
    And the mean riddle, How to tally
Reality with such appearance,
    When in the nearest valley

'Perhaps already she I sought,
    She, sought and seeker, had gone by,
And each of us in turn was trapped
    By simple treachery.

'The evening brought a field, a wood.
    I left behind the hills of lies,
And watched beside a mouldering gate
    A deer with its rock-crystal eyes.

'On either pillar of the gate
    A deer's head watched within the stone.
The living deer with quiet look
    Seemed to be gazing on

'Its pictured death—and suddenly
   I knew, Diotima was dead,
As if a single thought had sprung
   From the cold and the living head.

'That image held me and I saw
   All moving things so still and sad,
But till I came into the mountains
   I know I was not mad.

'What made the change? The hills and towers
   Stood otherwise than they should stand,
And without fear the lawless roads
   Ran wrong through all the land.

'Upon the swarming towns of iron
   The bells hailed down their iron peals,
Above the iron bells the swallows
   Glilded on iron wheels.

'And there I watched in one confounded
   The living and the unliving head.
Why should it be? For now I know
   Diotima was dead

'Before I left the starting place;
   Empty the course, the garland gone,
And all that race as motionless
   As these two heads of stone,'

So Hölderlin mused for thirty years
   On a green hill by Tübingen,
Dragging in pain a broken mind
   And giving thanks to God and men.

Inevitably one finds reactions to and sympathy with Hölderlin as one of the most durable modern poets. This impression of his poetry is confirmed and reinforced if we keep in mind that the German poet was a serious student and scholar of the Greek and Roman classics:

> From the first his mind was possessed by the classical world,
> and Greece in particular, with its gods and its elements, fire,
> water, air, the ether. He lived in that world more exclusively

than any other modern poet has done. Then came his mental breakdown: grief for the loss of Susette Gontard shattered his mind, smashing his classical world to pieces.[13]

Muir thus chooses one of the figures he found himself most drawn to in his reading of foreign literatures—a figure who had already become a social legend and a figure worthy of the ballad form. Through identification with the nineteenth-century German, the poet counts on lasting along with Hölderlin; the fact that this expectation may be in some sense servile (enduring through the persona of Hölderlin) is compensated for by the "fact" of the poem itself.

Suffering in love, carried to the absolute breaking point, is the most dominant manifestation of archetypal knowledge provided by Edwin Muir in "Hölderlin's Journey." The poem has elements of magic and fantasy, yet it remains clear and lucid with respect to delineating the tragic situation. As in "The Enchanted Knight," Muir's opening explication presents an indication of the poem's thematic content. The essential dramatic situation is presented in the first four lines:

> When Hölderlin started from Bordeaux
> He was not mad but lost in mind,
> For time and space had fled away
> With her he had to find.

By using an $x \, a \, y \, a$ rhyme scheme and making $x \, y$ somewhat shorter than $a \, a$, the poet confirms formally our expectations for the ballad form. In this case what we might call the intellectual ballad is characterized by subject matter one might find as present in a university curriculum, a poem that a modern academic journal might publish, or a poem that does not stem out of the oral tradition with respect to its essential, predominant elements. In fact, all of these early ballads of Muir may be thought of as intellectual ballads, or perhaps art ballads.

Muir, like Poe, associates bells with a euphoric, hopeful, painful state of madness as the poem moves into its second stanza. The condition of loneliness—the absence of the loved one—is emphasized by the contrast with the distant sounds and also the "maze of little hills," which are not merely "head-high" but similar in stature. The poet is "journeying" through what could either be an imaginative landscape or a transmuted real one. A faint bell tolls at some central place where Hölderlin is not (at the wedding

13. *Essays on Literatures and Society* (Boston: Harvard University Press, 1965), p. 86.

or burial of his beloved). The hills are "emerald" —not only hard and valuable stone and reminiscent of wedding gems but also green, the color of jealousy or, as Lorca felt, of desire. The protagonist of the ballad experiences nothing of the actual physical presence of his mistress, the love object. Instead he comes upon the monotony of other hills:

> Too small to climb, too tall to show
> More than themselves, the hills lay round.

The hills are not only symbolic of a barren alternative to an actual or hypothetical love object or situation; they are seen to stretch also to infinity. Hölderlin, already "lost in mind," sees a multiplication of the situations inducing schizophrenia and suffering. Insofar as the events may suggest truth and something an individual might be seeking with passion, they are terrifyingly incomplete and nonsuggestive. Reality is bad enough, but appearances (such as the hills or the sounds) are even more distressful. Combinations of both the visual and the aural environment are intolerable. Hölderlin seeks an excuse for the love-fiasco, and tries to explain its failure through an apprehension of a possible set of circumstances that lifts the burden of moral guilt:

> 'Perhaps already she I sought,
>   She, sought and seeker, had gone by,
> And each of us in turn was trapped
>   By simple treachery.

Even in the realm of madness, life operates with peculiar justice, and a vision or imaginative state appears, almost as a reward for the searching, valid introspection of stanza 6. But the coin turns to the other side. The possible burial, mentioned in stanza 3, becomes a reality; the poet has experienced the death of the loved one, either in his own mind or in reality. The very gates of hell, the gentle living deer, and the designs of the deer in the gate, somehow or other might be identified with gentleness and pity. But these positive qualities are now horribly transmuted into something else at the gates of death. The scene seems to Hölderlin a mockery of himself and of his emotion—a rationalization for his ineptness (insofar as one can not love the dead in the flesh) and therefore torturously suspect; furthermore, death can be thought of as merely a simple fact conducive to emotions of sorrow. The poet continues his Gothic pilgrimage and journey—confirming his own madness and sensing at too close hand the evil things of life. In stanza 12 the four repetitions of the word "iron" are terrifying: we are reminded of a human being used as an anvil and being struck with a large iron hammer, This is the effect that Muir achieves through the depiction of the often frail human sensibility in relation to environment. Hölderlin is reminded of his lover. All that he has gone through is vain, and, as if mocking himself as a hyprocrite, the poet realizes that the journey was undertaken in spite of the foreknowledge of his achieving nothing. One often thinks in a rather perverse way of death in connection with one's most loved human beings—and the death theme, the too conscious wish for the death of others (even the loved one), adds to the almost total blackness of the devastated consciousness of the madman. Muir closes with an appropriate epitaph, one of the most serious and moving stanzas in English poetry:

> So Hölderlin mused for thirty years
>   On a green hill by Tübingen,
> Dragging in pain a broken mind
>   And giving thanks to God and men.

IV

Affirmation

One might suspect a pitiful or unmerciful weakness or flaw on the part of the poet if such tragic, terrifying manifestations were to continue in the love verse of Edwin Muir. The power and integrity of the pessimism are strong early. But these poems give way to much happier depictions of love; the early, unhappy documents remain to show us that the love harmony that the Orkneyman (or Scots peasant) captured was not accidental and was not easy to come by. The movement from failure in love to success in love corresponds to the way in life, often, that each succeeding love grows better for many people—at least with respect to particulars and over the long run. One difference between Muir and the Shakespeare of the *Sonnets* is that Muir is closer to depicting the fundamental emotion of love in isolation from suspected homosexuality or adultery. The speculations about a male love, a love for a courtesan, or an adulterous, illicit love which have surrounded many of the discussions of the *Sonnets* seem completely inapplicable to Muir's love poems. The sense of evil is conspicuously missing in the great middle love poems. In fact, Muir's own short and infrequent love verse is so moving and simple, and apparently so pure, that it is difficult to accuse the poet of any evil tendencies at all. These short structures are a tribute to the powers that are still possible for English poetry—and in their simple purity of feeling, chastity, clarity, and compassion they often rival, poem against poem, many of the *Sonnets* of Shakespeare.

To move from "Hölderlin's Journey" to "The Annunciation ('Now in this iron reign')"[1] of the 1943 volume *The Narrow Place*[2] is to span a sequence of poems where love themes are frequently used to bolster a poem's principal thematic content. In a poem depicting an area involved in war, "The Town Betrayed,"[3] we learn from the narrator that

1. "The Annunciation ('Now in this iron reign')," p. 117.

2. *The Narrow Place* (London: Faber, 1943).

3. "The Town Betrayed," pp. 76–77.

Our harlot daughters lean and watch
   The ships crammed down with shells and guns.

Like painted prows far out they lean:
   A world behind, a world before.
The leaves are covering up our hills,
   Neptune has locked the shore.

The corruption of the women is made worse by forces from without that threaten the best parts and vital experience of life. The male lover wanders in agony and isolation, never able to move back to the center of a fruitful love experience. The "shore" is "locked" (one thinks of stories of Orpheus and Eurydice); the man cannot come to the woman. He is powerless and corrupt like the women themselves, who can hold no real feeling because of the low condition of the men or fathers. The body politic freezes the grass-roots lovers. Such a societal situation gives way in "The Recurrence"[4] to a more fated conception of human love. In that poem Muir employs the "Seven Ages of Man" formula that Shakespeare used in "As You Like It," except that Muir sees four key periods and relates them to the doctrine of eternal recurrence:

All things return, Nietzsche said,
The ancient wheel revolves again,
Rise, take up your numbered fate;
The cradle and the bridal bed,
Life and the coffin wait.

The "wheel" is a very dominant image here, and its weight and tone linger on throughout the poem.

One might be accused of overinterpretation with respect to "The Grove"[5] if one were to attach too much significance to the "we" of the poem. Nevertheless someone (perhaps a divine and total woman) is accompanying the poet on his journey through time, places, and space, much as Beatrice had to accompany Dante in his imaginative trip to the realms of supernatural forms. What one is reminded of (to speak particularly as distinct from universally) is a lifelong wife, helper (in the modern sense of "helpmate"), companion, and easer of the burden of reality:

4. "The Recurrence," pp. 102–104.

5. "The Grove," pp. 108–109.

There was no road at all to that high place
But through the smothering grove,
Where as we went the shadows wove
Adulterous shapes of animal hate and love,
The idol-crowded nightmare Space,
Wood beyond wood, tree behind tree,
And every tree an empty face
Gashed by the casual lightning mark
The first great Luciferian animal
Scored on leaf and bark.
This was, we knew, the heraldic ground,
And therefore now we heard our footsteps fall
With the true legendary sound,
Like secret trampling behind a wall,
As if they were saying: To be: to be.

The "we" of lines 3, 11, and 12 of this segment of the poem involves our hope of being with someone as we face the maze of the archetypal, mythological, and perennial landscapes that might accompany us on the way to death. The feeling is not unlike the romantic reverie of a sensitive, adolescent youth who dreams of saving his fair lady from an imagined or actual disaster. The disaster in this case, however, is reality itself ("Scored" by Lucifer), or in a particular form, the area of black romance in lines 4 and 5. Such a reading, nevertheless, may be thought of as only one side of a two-sided coin. At the close of this poem, the grove (perhaps symbolizing a place of love, Eden, friendship, home, or marriage, or perhaps that of a chance encounter) is seen as a place of light as well as one of "smothering."

The sense of intimacy in "The Gate" is perhaps derived from our sense that we may be in contact with two young lovers. In the case of Muir's poem the sense of tragedy is purged out of existence. Perhaps we have two members of a family, or perhaps just two young companions. Really the situation might simply involve young people who have run away—or even who are merely outside a house, perhaps a house of the aristocracy. The sense of an enjoyed intimacy in spite of problems is similar to that of "The Grove":

We sat, two children, warm against the wall
Outside the towering stronghold of our fathers
That frowned its stern security down upon us.
We could not enter there. That fortress life,
Our safe protection, was too gross and strong
For our unpractised palates. Yet our guardians

Cherished our innocence with gentle hands,
(They, who had long since lost their innocence,)
And in grave play put on a childish mask
Over their tell-tale faces, as in shame
For the rich food that plumped their lusty bodies
And made them strange as gods. We sat that day
With that great parapet behind us, safe
As every day, yet outcast, safe and outcast
As castaways thrown upon an empty shore.
Before us lay the well-worn scene, a hillock
So small and smooth and green, it seemed intended
For us alone and childhood, a still pond
That opened upon no sight a quiet eye,
A little stream that tinkled down the slope.
But suddenly all seemed old
And dull and shrunken, shut within itself
In a sullen dream. We were outside, alone.
And then behind us the huge gate swung open.[6]

One is somehow reminded of the familiar theme of the setting loose of the child, as when the mother and father bird relinquish control of the young, taught them what they must know in order to get along in life. The parents may have the feeling that much more is to be gained through the young adult's independence than through further dependency. The possibilities outside of the family environment offer more, and the parents, through sympathy and instinct, hope for a mate for their child. On the other hand, part of the power of the poem resides in its suggestion that the care and safeguarding of the children are still foremost in the minds of the elders, and that the guardians are capable of help in case of danger, aware of how to provide for the safety of the younger people in spite of their new freedom. In other words, one has the sense of omnipresent protection on the part of the elders in relation to the truants. To judge the poem on another level, the parents, in spite of their godlike existences (in the eyes of the child outsider) still operate and act in a realm where they are able to judge correctly what the scope of freedom of a pair of vagrants should be. However, since it is "behind" the pair that the "huge gate swung open," there is something almost sinister and dark in the parents' movement and actions. Perhaps it is mere chance, or perhaps some evil threat to the two children's intimacy, their present freedom, or a highly special, hypothetical, future, and ultimate freedom. One cannot help but be reminded of the cultural

6. "The Gate," p. 110.

heritage of certain members of western European culture, and the task that is therefore placed on the shoulders of their children. "The Gate" may be thought of as cultural as well as familial.

At this point it is appropriate to restore the balance by discussing five great love poems which are in sharp contrast to the earlier poems' bits and pieces of despairing and complicated love. These five poems, which unsentimentally depict fulfilled love, loom as prime achievements, and must be considered as central in the body of Muir's work. They are "The Annunciation ('Now in this iron reign'),"[7] "The Confirmation,"[8] "The Commemoration,"[9] "Song" ('Why should your face')[10] and "For Ann Scott-Moncrieff".[11]

In "The Annunciation" the conditions—set forth stanza by stanza—of closeness, of mutual giving, of simultaneous deification, and of a complete wholeness take their place in Muir's excellent conception of human and realized love:

The Annunciation

Now in this iron reign
I sing the liberty
Where each asks from each
What each most wants to give
And each awakes in each
What else would never be,
Summoning so the rare
Spirit to breathe and live.

Then let us empty out
Our hearts until we find
The last least trifling toy,
Since now all turns to gold,
And everything we have
Is wealth of heart and mind,
That squandered thus in turn
Grows with us manifold.

7. "The Annunciation ('Now in this iron reign')," p. 117.

8. "The Confirmation," p. 118.

9. "The Commemoration," pp. 118–119.

10. "Song ('Why should your face')," pp. 146–147.

11. "For Ann Scott-Moncrieff (1914–1943)," pp. 156–157.

Giving, I'd give you next
Some more than mortal grace,
But that you deifying
Myself I might deify,
Forgetting love was born
Here in a time and place,
And robbing by such praise
This life we magnify.

Whether the soul at first
This pilgrimage began,
Or the shy body leading
Conducted soul to soul
Who knows? This is the most
That soul and body can,
To make us each for each
And in our spirit whole.

In the "iron reign" of love—in a close, intimate relationship—one can see always irritating problems connected with independence and mutual liberty. But in the first stanza Muir lightens the burden of these problems by simply singing of the freedom in which "each asks from each/What each most wants to give." In the poem, idealistic as it is, the lovers act only in relationship to one another with respect to the pattern of their wishes, desires, and instincts. The solution in the poem is as simple as that. The single person, the single "other," is sufficient in that that person provides and conjures up as an entity all that could be wanted. What is desired makes of the other person the appropriate self—and the whole process of "drawing out" is simple, adequate, and elemental—"Summoning so the rare/Spirit to breathe and live." The gifts to each other include "The last least trifling toy," so that

everything we have
Is wealth of heart and mind,
That squandered thus in turn
Grows with us manifold.

In a dazzling series of images and thoughts in the third stanza, the protagonist and lover moves to consider the deification of the loved one. In danger of a cheap slickness and overproliferation, the poet reminds us that love "was born/Here in a time and place," and that even the most skillful, excellent, and great praise is an injustice to the relationship's true scope, brilliance, and nature. We would be "robbing by such praise This life we magnify." The poem could end here—but the poet instead moves on to a fourth and final stanza. Taking up a facet of the traditional body-soul archetype, the poet, in a sense, sees the old arguments, the old dichotomy, as misleading. Both soul and body together "make us each for each/And in our spirit whole." Muir is at his best in a poem like this, which fuses his reflective capacity, his sensitivity, and his great depth with one of the adequate and significant emotions—love. "The Annunciation" of "the other" is resolved through argumentative and idealistic acceptance of the single and adequate love object. The poem reminds us of the story of Dante and Beatrice in the *Divine Comedy*, but set in modern terms.

"The Confirmation" is similar to and vies with "The Annunciation" in its qualitative tone of an achieved, central, and manifested human love:

The Confirmation

Yes, yours, my love, is the right human face.
I in my mind had waited for this long,
Seeing the false and searching for the true,
Then found you as a traveller finds a place
Of welcome suddenly amid the wrong
Valleys and rocks and twisting roads. But you,
What shall I call you? A fountain in a waste,
A well of water in a country dry,
Or anything that's honest and good, an eye
That makes the whole world bright. Your open heart,
Simple with giving, gives the primal deed,
The first good world, the blossom, the blowing seed,
The hearth, the steadfast land, the wandering sea,
Not beautiful or rare in every part,
But like yourself, as they were meant to be.

One might speak of a high poetic language appropriate to the emotion of love—in modern terms, the language of John Crowe Ransom's "The Equilibrists" and Ezra Pound's "Cino." In traditional terms it is the language of Baudelaire in "A une Dame Créole," Robert Desnos in "Le Paysage," Yeats in almost every poem, Donne in the metaphysical love poems such as "Song ('Sweetest love, I do not goe')," Schiller in "Der Handschuh," and most noticeably, Shakespeare in the *Sonnets*. In this type of "upper-range" or "high" poetic language, the feeling of the poet and the tone of the poem are perhaps more central than the language—what we recognize immediately is the feeling or emotion of the lover. Then, going along with this, the language has a certain sparse, opaque, and luminescent quality—general, yet particular, in its scope. Usually it is not symbolic, but it is direct, clear, and often simple in its nature. The imagery is economic but attractive. The dominant tone or feeling is simple—no more or less than the ample depiction of human love with language as the artistic material. It is perhaps more difficult to describe than to see—and one can see this type of language in "The Confirmation."

Much of the poem's power and strength must reside in its being what one might call a long sonnet—one of fifteen lines instead of fourteen. The fact that the reader is used to fourteen lines (and is often put off or distracted by the formal elaboration of this scheme) perhaps explains the way that Muir's simple language grasps the reader's attention so much more completely than in many of the other poems. Also, perhaps the reason that the poet begins rather unnoticeably in a tercet variation—*a b c, a b c*—has something to do with the poem's attraction. Often an irregularity in rhyme is justified simply because it is, or works—perhaps this is the only explanation of the effectiveness of the relatively irregular *c a d d e f f f e f* ending.

Yet even more central than these phenomena is the use of "rightness" coupled with love as the governing idea of the poem. We often hear "You haven't met the right person yet" or "How lucky you are to have met the right person." The idea behind such expressions is that for each human being there is another person of the opposite sex who is somehow "the most right person," or even "definitely the right one," for somebody. Following "The Annunciation ('Now in this iron reign')" in the Oxford text, "The Confirmation" strikes ground in an area where externals have already been cleared away. And in the final line the latter poem stakes a high claim, as objects of reality are seen as "Not beautiful or rare in every part/ But like yourself, as they were meant to be." The compliment extends beyond the boundaries of mere personal beauty itself to encompass the whole person—both body and soul. The beautiful is not ruled out—in fact one suspects it is present—but what we have here is something more complete, encompassing the entire being of the poetic lover and his woman. In fact, the suggestion extends even beyond the lovers; the environment itself can be thought of as transfigured.

The third poem in this triadic succession in the 1965 Oxford text is "The Commemoration", a poem as stunningly successful and relevant as "The Confirmation" and "The Annunciation."

The Commemoration

I wish I could proclaim
My faith enshrined in you
And spread among a few

Our high but hidden fame,
That we new life have spun
Past all that's thought and done,
And someone or no one
Might tell both did the same.

Material things will pass
And we have seen the flower
And the slow falling tower
Lie gently in the grass,
But meantime we have stored
Riches past bed and board
And nursed another hoard
Than callow lad and lass.

Invisible virtue now
Expands upon the air
Although no fruit appear
Nor weight bend down the bough,
And harvests truly grown
For someone or no one
Are stored and safely won
In hollow heart and brow.

How can one thing remain
Except the invisible,
The echo of a bell
Long rusted in the rain?
This strand we weave into
Our monologue of two,
And time cannot undo
That strong and subtle chain.

The acts of mutual love serve as a source of faith in another person's being: so strong and successful is this love that it may be thought of as enshrined —a basic assumption of the poem. The poet desires to "spread among a few" their "high but hidden fame"; instead of a boisterous, egocentric view of their love of each other, the lovers are careful to hide parts of their relationship. Yet in spite of this the poet has captured the essence and nature of this love in his verse; in this sense it is an already famous love story, but still hidden until history discovers this poem, which thus serves simultaneously as a device of modesty and as an agent of permanent acclaim. The poet-lover feels that he and his partner have "new life" "spun/

Past all that's thought and done" (one of Muir's best lines). He goes on to close the stanza, claiming that "someone or no one/Might tell both did the same." It is accurate to say in summing up this ending of the stanza that "The love was good—watch it as you will."

In stanza 2 we move from intangible, unpermanent things to a contrasting condition where the lovers "have stored Riches past bed and board." At the beginning of stanza 3 the external environment is itself transfigured through the worth and value of the lovers—a familiar idea in Muir. The love now commemorated is untainted by the reality and weight of original sin. The lovers are spoken of in terms of harvest, safety, and victory. Love is seen as something real, important, and rich in spite of metaphysical or existential nothingness. The final triumph is over time:

> And time cannot undo
> That strong and subtle chain.

As if in philosophic explanation for the dazzling and successful middle love period, in contrast to the earlier, less happy times, Muir wrote "Song ('Why should your face')," where in each stanza there is an intrusion upon the "single song of two." Perhaps Muir wanted to convey the impression of a lack of sentimentality to go along with his achieved, full love feelings; italicizing the passages of more ponderous, cloudy implication may be of some use. If he was being on the safe side with respect to sentimentality, then he chose an adequate occasion:

Song

> Why should your face so please me
> *That if one little line should stray*
> *Bewilderment would seize me*
> *And drag me down the tortuous way*
> *Out of the noon into the night?*
> But so, into this tranquil light
> You raise me.

> How could our minds so marry
> *That, separate, blunder to and fro,*
> *Make for a point, miscarry,*
> *And blind as headstrong horses go?*
> Though now they in their promised land
> At pleasure travel hand in hand
> Or tarry.

This concord is an answer
To questions far beyond our mind
Whose image is a dancer.
All effort is to ease refined
Here, *weight* is light; this is the dove
Of love and peace, not heartless love
The lancer.

And yet I still must wonder
That such an armistice can be
And *life roll by in thunder*
To leave this calm with you and me.
This tranquil voice of silence, yes,
This single song of two, this is
A wonder.

The emotion of love, in its utmost delicacy and tenderness, can be based on something quite small, or, on the other hand, be jarred to nonexistence at the slightest provocation—this is the significance of "if one little line should stray/Bewilderment would seize me." In the next stanza the condition of success in love is established definitely. The minds of the love object and the poetic lover are seen as being able to marry in spite of obstacles. In reading the third stanza, if we think of the bird of Yeats's "Sailing to Byzantium," we can compare—or more appropriately, contrast—its nature with that of Muir's "dove." In Yeats the bird is symbolic of permanence in the face of old age, and suggestive of permanence in art in the face of time. In Muir the bird appropriately is "the dove/Of love and peace, not heartless love/The lancer"; it symbolizes love's reconciliations and its highest manifestations of shared sympathies and quiet, natural, unpremeditated joys. In contrast to life, which rolls by "in thunder," we find Muir's beautiful expression:

This tranquil voice of silence, yes,
This single song of two, this is
A wonder.

The effects of the poem on the reader, along with the simplicity of the poem's title, remind one that there are experiences even more valuable than American popular music or even the older tradition of the European song.

Some of Muir's dominant ideas are very simple and yet, at the same

time, very profound. In the case of "For Ann Scott-Moncrieff (1914–1943)"
it appears as if the premature death of "a woman young," and an accompanying sense of regret on the part of a poet, combined to produce a
moving elegy or eulogy (as one might look at it). Instead of mourning the
death of a male friend, Muir mourns the death of a young woman; but it is
not sorrow that is characteristic of the poem, but rather a depiction of the
"beautiful virtues" of the girl. What we have is not unlike the medieval
courtly formula. Death serves not as an occasion for mourning, but rather
as an opportunity to sum up what was best about the person when he or
she was alive. An interesting thematic feature that serves to bind the poem
together involves a kind of coupling of like concepts at the beginning and
end of each stanza. In the first stanza, we find the word "die" at the beginning and the word "Death" at the end; in stanza 2, "You who were Ann
much more/Than others are that or this," and "And are entirely Ann." In
the final stanza, natural conditions are stressed: it begins with "the years'
assaults," and "last summer" is mentioned in the final line. As the poem
progresses we become aware of the limitations of immortality, now that
the actual physical presence of the girl has vanished. Her great beauty is
now inaccessible (again a very medieval concept). In the second stanza we
become aware of the girl's intellectual beauty through the poet's awareness of

> What you once used to say
> Of the great Why and How,
> On that or the other day?

Her physical grace and the beauty of her sensibility occurred in spite of the
fact that

> You too had the faults
> That Emily Brontë had,
> Ills of body and soul,
>
> . . . .
> Yet 'the world is a pleasant place'
> I can hear your voice repeat,

Muir implies that she has a kind of stature in spite of adversity. Muir, an
observant poet, was not accidental in choosing Princes Street, Edinburgh's
main thoroughfare, as an image of place for the poem: the name in itself
is beautiful and was there waiting to be used. The name "Scott-Moncrieff"
may also call into play for readers the C. K. Scott Moncrieff translation of
Proust's *Remembrance of Things Past*. That work is in its English transla-

tion a prose masterpiece, and a work masterfully autonomous in itself. Muir appeals here to our sense of what a child or relative of the translator would be like; as in the poem "princely prize," "chambered brow," "your heritage," and "extravagant" all suggest a child of the aristocracy or upper classes—the classes which often produce the most attractive offspring.

What is not said about love is as important as what is said in two of Muir's poems, which are possibly about love more by implication than by the nature of their metaphors or their imagistic content. These poems are "The Ring"[12] and "All We."[13] In "The Ring," it is true, Muir is discussing a kind of Adamic condition at points in the poem. At some time in the past there were few problems from without and few from within. The Edenic state is seen to linger on in the present as a kind of dream of something to be hoped for again. It can serve therapeutic use in our own dreams, suggesting an intellectual alternative to a battle-torn present environment. Part of the power of "The Ring"—which suggests the marriage ring—resides in the fact that what may be being talked about is not just a particular environment, but a kind of wholesome past with respect to male and female relationships. Animals are, however, predominant in this poem. We are in a poetic territory that is an ultimate starting point for man. Man is seen as coming out of a matrix of forces in the animal world—a world where "they/Had never known the vow and the pilgrimage." "The Ring" or the marriage ring can be seen here as something which may separate us from the animals and be a vital step in evolution; thereby the poem is involved with Muir's poetic examination of love.

"All We" deals on a simpler plane with a simple phenomenon, and does so deeply and directly. Man, the inventor, the arbiter, makes "Things transitory and good" and therefore enjoys what is around him—both things that are fashioned by man and things he comes into contact with that are not fashioned by men. Even objects in the latter category show evidence of "the maker's solicitude." We are conscious of these graces, or glimmerings of immortality, or glimpses of merciful fashioning. We know and recognize "the delicacy/Of bringing shape to birth."

> To fashion the transitory
> We gave and took the ring
> And pledged ourselves to the earth.

12. "The Ring," p. 113.

13. "All We," p. 158.

Through marriage, the marriage ceremony, the marriage ring—through the very fact of marriage—we are pledged to both procreation and ultimate union.

In "Time Held in Time's Despite,"[14] the theme is the common one of love in some sense defying time. The lovers are in a state of possession of "what time has made/Our very own in our and time's despite." The nature of the possession is really what love has made and residued between the man and the woman (or friends or the human race, to read literally). Ending beautifully, Muir asserts more directly that

> 'Impersonally soul and soul embrace,
>
> And incorruptibly are bodies bound.'
> The hours that melt like snowflakes one by one
> Leave us this residue, this virgin ground
> For ever fresh, this firmament and this sun.
>
> Then let us lay unasking hand in hand,
> And take our way, thus led, into our land.

To speak in a special sense, it is the love between two people that posits something worth while enough to consider existence as a valuable time. In a way, love is the purified Garden of Eden from which man steps into the new land "hand in hand" with someone else. A sense of burden and difficulty gives way to better enterprises. In "Love in Time's Despite,"[15] Muir states his problem in the first four lines, particularly in the first sentence:

> You who are given to me to time were given
> Before through time I stretched my hand to catch
> Yours in the flying race. Oh we were driven
> By rivalry of him who has no match.

The common enough conception of a life or existence in an immortal realm of which we have no memory here receives a romantic transmutation in the hands of the thoughtful poet. The historical and prehistorical lovers are seen as loved by what seems to be a deity. In the poem man is not alone but with a member of the opposite sex (probably)—his wife or life-partner

14. "Time Held in Time's Despite," p. 155.

15. "Love in Time's Despite," p. 193.

—both out of time and in time. In either of the latter cases the ultimate
ruler is "subtle and keen as thought" and "has no care" for the love partner.
The lovers are seen to defy time and its ruler—daring

> To keep in his despite our summer still,
> Which flowered, but shall not wither, at his will.

Thus the gift of love is seen in ultimate terms with respect to its possible
origins—and it is seen in a condition of freedom, for the ultimate deity implied here is not likely to move the pair backwards or hold them in the
present. Thus "Time Held in Time's Despite" delves into one of the richest
possibilities of love in time—its actual nature; and "Love in Time's Despite"
discusses love in its relationship to broad metaphysical questions concerning
the individual's relationship to history, the universe, and a possible deity.

"Love's Remorse"[16] takes up the specific older problem of the decay of
physical beauty and perhaps of intelligence—both with respect to the on-
slaught of old age, and in a more suggestive sense (perhaps a modern one)
the laceration of female beauty by the male lover. However, in the strict
context of the poem it is time that works the crime. The male—the leader
in love—is frustrated by the simple inability on his part to stop the terrifying process of time. In lines 9 through 12 we are slightly heartened by the
metaphysical reassertion of a "true love":

> But the old saw still by the heart retold,
> 'Love is exempt from time.' And that is true.
> But we, the loved and the lover, we grow old;
> Only the truth, the truth is always new:

The "old saw" represents the wisdom of the ages that transcends particular
problems in a strange and often inhospitable world. The fact that "Love is
exempt from time" at least gives some basis for living. Yet, as the poet says,
"we, the loved and the lover, we grow old." Of what avail is it that we are
always encountering new territory, new terrains, and new truths? There is
only one solution. Our lover like most men has been crushed and must
turn to religion. However, in this case, it is a saving thought which main-
tains dignity, and at the same time, human power:

> 'Eternity alone our wrong can right,
> That makes all young again in time's despite.'

16. "Love's Remorse," pp. 192-193.

Other poems such as "Circle and Square"[17] and "Head and Heart"[18] deal, respectively, with mutual individuality in love and with the way that problems and pain in love sink into the past. In the latter case we reach a condition where "all our sorrow" is "a memory." The "Annunciation ('The angel and the girl are met')"[19] deals sensitively with the love of an angel for a girl, and provides mythical metaphor or therapy, and possibly a moral pattern, for young men concerned with love of young women. The theme of young lovers—particularly poets and great, beautiful women—is brought out in the first stanza of "Orpheus' Dream."[20] The poem also provides a pleasant mythical variant in that Orpheus and Eurydice, finally eternally united, are able to look back on "the poor ghost." "In Love for Long"[21] combines metaphysical searching with the search for an ultimate love. In the strictest sense the poem deals with a man's search and love for a god; yet we are also reminded of the individual's search for a love object. "Dream and Thing"[22] has at least two themes: that reality eventually shapes itself according to our dreams, and that after a reality is manifested, we are able to read the details; the "reality" could be a reality of love. A poem like "The Incarnate One"[23] deals with the historical crisis of an overly puritanical antisensualism:

> Abstract calamity, save for those who can
> Build their cold empire on the abstract man.

Quoting from "The Island,"[24] a comparatively late poem from *One Foot in Eden*,[25] is a most appropriate means of closing the discussion of love in Edwin Muir's poetry.

17. "Circle and Square," pp. 191–192.

18. "Head and Heart," p. 181.

19. "The Annunciation ('The angel and the girl are met')," pp. 223–224.

20. "Orpheus' Dream," pp. 216–217.

21. "In Love for Long," pp. 159–160.

22. "Dream and Thing," p. 242.

23. "The Incarnate One," pp. 228–229.

24. "The Island," pp. 248–249.

25. *One Foot in Eden* (London: Faber, 1956).

Though come a different destiny,
Though fall a universal wrong
More stern than simple savagery,
Men are made of what is made,
The meat, the drink, the life, the corn,
Laid up by them, in them reborn.
And self-begotten cycles close
About our way; indigenous art
And simple spells make unafraid
The haunted labyrinths of the heart,
And with our wild succession braid
The resurrection of the rose.

V

Personae

Our concern in this chapter will sometimes be with Edwin Muir's own attitude in particular poems; but mostly we will examine the characters he presumes to speak for, the forms of his poetic individualism. We will be able to see that Muir's map of personae is wide and very rich indeed—as well as very diverse in its specific details. In fact one might speak of all the poems in the 1965 Oxford text[1]—from the first one, "Childhood,"[2] to "'I Have Been Taught,'"[3] the last one—as maps of Muir's identity or identities. In short, there are sufficient grounds for a complex and varied understanding of Edwin Muir. There is a basis for expanding our awareness of the dynamics of personae, as well as for a heightened understanding of specific historical or legendary characters—and therefore of world literature. We find a means of expanding our range of sympathy and tolerance. The choice of figures from world literature often allows strictly comparative approaches.

The "Ballad of Hector in Hades"[4] provides an opportunity to see how Muir uses a particular epic personage, or persona, to add a variant to a relatively common, shared myth. The poem also works out Muir's personal conflict, or feeling of guilt, about the act of writing. Finally, the narrative acts somehow to make the historical personae exist in a poetic territory that is less terrible, less tragic, less painful than the most common version of the myth. In Muir's poem, Hector, as a character, may be thought of as having been elevated from a lesser condition to one more

1. *Collected Poems* (New York: Oxford University Press, 1965).

2. "Childhood," p. 19.

3. "'I Have Been Taught,'" p. 302.

4. "Ballad of Hector in Hades," p. 24–26.

fraught with possibility in the hands of the poet-mythmaker. The first
stanza is a post mortem; the setting in time occurs after the battle of
Hector and Achilles:

> Yes, this is where I stood that day,
> Beside this sunny mound.
> The walls of Troy are far away,
> And outward comes no sound.

Muir assumes that the events of the *Iliad* are in the reader's mind; what
occurs is a kind of reenactment of the real events,[5] performed rather ease-
fully by Hector. In his "painted world" of pure form, in his immortal territory, Hector sees out of the side of one eye, as it were, the race and the
painful conclusion:

> And in that space our shadows run,
> His shadow there and mine,

and

> Two shadows racing on the grass,
> Silent and so near,
> Until his shadow falls on mine.
> And I am rid of fear.

The pain and tragedy become justified, in one sense, in that Hector is now
in a superior condition where the real world has been left behind. Hector is
using his immortal imagination, as it were. The poet, by presenting this
variant, takes account of his sensitivity; the feeling of Muir when reading
the *Iliad* is similar to that of many other people in that he wonders why
the tragedy of Hector and Troy and the Greeks is occurring at all. The poet
feels guilty even about historical events he is only remotely connected with.
Through the assertion and creation of his ghost, Muir acts out a kind of
salvation drama to rid himself of the terrible burden of guilt. And finally
Hector himself suffers a "sea change," and emerges as a more romantic
figure than a tragic one—perhaps a superior view in a period of history

---

5. This is one possible interpretation of the setting of the poem. One might argue well that
the last stanza indicates that the opening stanza speaks of Hector just as he is about to go into
battle with Achilles. With this interpretation in mind the last stanza indicates the end of the
battle; Hector is "far away" and just at this point dead. This poem, like "In Love for Long"
and "Dream and Thing," works well with either one of two possible interpretations.

such as ours characterized by nervous breakdowns stemming out of feelings
of personal guilt.

If the long and developed soliloquies of Shakespeare's Falstaff throughout
some of the historical plays are welcomed as providing an intimate, realized
portrait of a character not drawn from the nobility or royalty itself, then
Muir's "A Trojan Slave"[6] is to be welcomed with respect to its terms of
portrayal: a slave drawn probably from the ordinary, common classes of
fallen Troy. What we are dealing with is an ancient common man. In this
case, Muir's choice of a persona partially satisfies our inevitable curiosity
about people separate from recorded history. The picture presented is not a
happy one. Yet some profound examinations of currents and ripples of
political and social behavior in Troy are presented. Most importantly, from
a moral point of view, we have a person who was a minor actor in the general scene regretting the episode of the Trojan War in human history. Up to
this point the poem is like much of Muir's early verse; but the Trojan
episode seems only part of a more general disillusionment with life itself—
not because of a reduced situation or sense of regret, but rather because of
a more general, philosophical pessimism stemming out of much experience
with lived realities:

> I lost a sword in a forgotten fight,
> And ever since my arm has been too light
> For this dense world, and shall grow lighter still.

The impression we have is of a world-weary man past the prime of life
who speaks in inconspicuous couplets so as to disguise his scorn and
contempt for what life has brought to him. He speaks of his "rage," but
from the point of view of a weary intellectual:

> Yet through that rage shines Troy's untroubled hill,
> And many a tumbled wall and vanished tree
> Remains, as if in spite, a happy memory.

A note of idealism is sounded with respect to the past of Troy. Yet the
slave still clings with a kind of personal carelessness to the memories
that have emerged from Troy's destruction. He spites himself with his
fancy in this rather unhappy, forlorn way.

One may speak of the poet as a magic maker, a musician with words.
Muir's use of the medieval persona of Merlin for his own philosophic

6. "A Trojan Slave," pp. 72–73.

purposes is striking. The poet—a writing poet—realizes that in spite of what he can create that contributes to general goodness, he may still be misinterpreted and lead someone to an evil action. That is not the only problem. The poet may believe that what he has written is "the right thing" or "highly moral"; but in a world of furtive knowledge his poetic act may, in point of fact, be evil in itself. In response to these problems, Muir wrote about a character who is usually depicted as evil—an overreacher. Muir at least acknowledges some consciousness of proper intention in someone who may be a historical victim:

Merlin

O Merlin in your crystal cave
Deep in the diamond of the day,
Will there ever be a singer
Whose music will smooth away
The furrow drawn by Adam's finger
Across the meadow and the wave?
Or a runner who'll outrun
Man's long shadow driving on,
Break through the gate of memory
And hang the apple on the tree?
Will your magic ever show
The sleeping bride shut in her bower,
The day wreathed in its mound of snow
And Time locked in his tower?

Muir almost says that in spite of savior after savior in man's history, in spite of victim after victim of evil, in spite of the efforts of countless men and women in thirty historical centuries, evil and problems still remain with the human race. Perhaps letting poets or artists back in "The Republic" might help the artist try to answer Muir's question.

"Then" presents a kind of unusual collective persona for the human race before that race even existed. The scene presented may be thought of as that of a prehistorical era where animals themselves may have had no consciousness at all but were merely mechanical monsters of force and destruction. Muir may even be speaking of and imaginatively realizing a primitive period that archeologists, anthropologists, scientists, or historians have no record of—but that may still survive in world myth and lore.

Then

There were no men and women then at all,
But the flesh lying alone,
And angry shadows fighting on a wall
That now and then sent out a groan
Buried in lime and stone,
And sweated now and then like tortured wood
Big drops that looked yet did not look like blood.

And yet as each drop came a shadow faded
And left the wall.
There was a lull
Until another in its shadow arrayed it,
Came, fought and left a blood-mark on the wall;
And that was all; the blood was all.

If there had been women there they might have wept
For the poor blood, unowned, unwanted,
Blank as forgotten script.
The wall was haunted
By mute maternal presences whose sighing
Fluttered the fighting shadows and shook the wall
As if that fury of death itself were dying.

If we think of something evolving from man, and of the shadows being shadows of present man, we become aware of one possible direction of interpretation. However, the strict historical interpretation seems most fruitful as the complicated logic of the poem develops. The shadows and groans may be thought of as those monsters in combat by a wall (in this case a natural stone formation); ·the battle continues among different animals fighting; in addition to the "lime and stone" the shadows are also blood-marked. It is useful to keep in mind the old Greek idea of men coming from a race of giants (as well as modern ideas about the eras of the dinosaurs). One can also imagine animal life of which we have no record of what may be vital links in the very distant evolutionary process. This suggestion, as well as the consciousness of the mysteries still surrounding particular aspects of human evolution, helps to add to the poem's relevance in that we are in the area or environment in the poem of a very distant time. The suggestion is perhaps that the blood of something fighting may be a source material of the human organism. This suggestion, rather "crackpottish" in itself, furnishes the basis for the poem's fundamental recognition. If the organic material involved in the formation of man were part of the blood of animals—or of something—then man comes from a rather terroristic background. However, if reacting to blood or shadows we find "mute maternal presences," or their organisms, then perhaps we can hold some hope for the future of man in that he came out of some basic material that, at its organic or sublogical level, was reacting against something that was the result and product of evil strife. Even if nothing happened except perhaps making it easier for humans to die, a good end would have been served. As I see it, the persona of this poem about the early human race is animal organism itself.

Edwin Muir uses "The Face"[7] as an occasion for agonizing introspection. The poet "begs" the reader to

> See me with all the terrors on my roads,
> The crusted shipwrecks rotting in my seas,
> And the untroubled oval of my face
> That alters idly with the moonlike modes
> And is unfathomably framed to please
> And deck the angular bone with passing grace.

In a hostile, destructive world, the poet sees himself as indifferent, capable of destruction, terrorized, and wavering from one thing to another. The purpose of this poem is obviously different from "Merlin"; the latter poem gave the fictive person the benefit of the doubt. (It is characteristic of Muir that he should be more generous to another person than to himself.) The man with the face carries the burden of accidental bluntness and old evils in his very person. The "untroubled oval" of the poet's face implies indifference, implies that the speaker is likely to go along with anything— whether good or evil or destructive in nature. "Unfathomably" suggests that the man with the face does not really know what he is doing because it is impossible to understand life and existence completely. It is a face designed to give mere petty small pleasures. The poet's negligible function is to cover up an unaesthetic moment—something dissonant and unembraceable. In passivity the poet will worry little about positive change; he will worry little about preserving the best:

7. "The Face," p. 106.

> I should have worn a terror-mask, should be
> A sight to frighten hope and faith away,
> Half charnel field, half battle and rutting ground.
> Instead I am a smiling summer sea
> That sleeps while underneath from bound to bound
> The sun and star-shaped killers gorge and play.

One is reminded of the legendary masks of Greek tragedy.

In "The Little General,"[8] as if in a partial response to the necessity of checking reality and holding it at bay, Muir deals courageously with a subject that certainly appears as if it would not be as popular with readers as that of other poems. The general is little, like most of the readers, because he is just a man. "Little" coupled with "General" carries with it the sense of a slight mockery of the persona. He is contemptible because he is only a minor puppet, a pawn in a vast universe—an example of the so-called modern man, setting out every day within the boundaries of his old life, and sometimes new life. Muir is talking about the "hard" element in the face of pettiness and the burdensome problems of life. We can make practical use of the myth of the "little General" to live our lives with a certain courage and tough stamina in the face of adversity and turns of bad luck. The poem ostensibly deals with hunting; the hunter comes "across the sound, bringing the island death." The familiar ritualistic behavior of hunter and hunted begins; the usual results ensue, with men victorious over the other terrestrial animals:

> Up on the hill a remnant of a tower
>   Had watched that single scene for many a year,
>
> Weaving a wordless tale where all were gathered
>   (Hunter and quarry and watcher and fabulous field),
> A sylvan war half human and half feathered,
>   Perennial emblem painted on the shield
>
> Held up to cow a never-conquered land
> Fast in the little General's fragile hand.

The victory is a victory of the man over the feathered creature; in a sense, it is a victory of man over a segment of nature; it is the same type of

8. "The Little General," pp. 110–111.

victory as that of a ruler or rulers over people. Yet, in a modern spirit to be
sure, Muir reminds us that the act may produce some goodness (taming the
otherwise doomed creatures or ·staying securely within the realms of
victory through personal control) and some problems (the "never-conquered
land" and "the little General's *fragile* hand"). Perhaps more modern is the
pride of man in his victories over other animals—a sense of well-being
through mutual mastery of a particular small realm of action. Yet it is too
early to speak of an ultimate victory; our uneasiness at this fact is more
modern than is the act of vanquishing the animals.

"The Old Gods" is one of Muir's clearest and most beautiful poems; the
sparseness of the language contributes to our focusing on the principal
theme: a poet addressing gods that are no longer in ascendancy. One has
the sense that it is the vanquished deities of Rome and Greece of which the
poet is speaking. To Muir, or the voice of Muir, that the gods should
enter our consciousness at all seems an act of mercy. The fact that we
remain conscious of them at all seems to indicate that they occupy a lower
station than they should—they have "never found eternity." The poem
demonstrates Muir's greatest virtue—real action (writing the poem) and
sympathy (the sentiment of the poem) on behalf of those who have fallen
on bad times:

The Old Gods

Old gods and goddesses who have lived so long
Through time and never found eternity,
Fettered by wasting wood and hollowing hill,

You should have fled our ever-dying song.
The mound, the well, and the green trysting tree,
They are forgotten, yet you linger still.

Goddess of caverned breast and channelled brow
And cheeks slow hollowed by millenial tears,
Forests of autumns fading in your eyes,

Eternity marvels at your counted years
And kingdoms lost in time, and wonders how
There could be thoughts so bountiful ·and wise

As yours beneath the ever-breaking bough,
And vast compassion curving like the skies.

In the first six lines of the sonnet, the poet presents a general statement. The fact that in line 7 the poet turns to a secular goddess rather than a god is pleasing; most of our later gods are masculine rather than feminine. The sonnet form is combined with the act of prayer; even more remarkably, the prayer and sonnet are applied to our sense of archaic and ancient mythologies. One often has a sense of guilt with respect to the demise of gods; and our sharing in Muir's poetic ritual-prayer helps appease these feelings. This easing of the burden of guilt in relationship to the demise of something is an illustration of how the poet, like the modern psychiatrist, alleviates the destructive guilt feelings present in the human sensibility. Without being romancers, poets such as Wallace Stevens (who somehow or other increases our delight in little things) and Jorge Guillen (who in *Cántico* erects great Spanish structures to ease our relationship to metaphysical truths) can be seen as close to Muir in acting out poetic rituals that reduce the shocks of life. In Muir's case the poems, as just demonstrated in part of "The Old Gods," invite our reason to operate more fully in a realm that might be described as "romantic" (in the sense of Greek romances or Shakespeare's *The Winter's Tale*) rather than "tragic" (in the sense of the development of *King Lear*). The suggestion in Muir's poem of "The mound, the well, and the green trysting tree," seems to be that quasi-religious functions or ideas centered on these objects are somehow less than our ideas centered on the divinities as people, or individuals in nature. The lines

> Goddess of caverned breast and channelled brow
> And cheeks slow hollowed by millenial tears,

bring up physical characteristics that are hard to argue about as anything less than essential. Combined with the peripheral idea of the poetic muse, they become even more central, relevant and delightful. These beautifully realized poetical images serve to draw us to Muir's goddess in a series of affirmations, and make us more amenable, by means of simple sexual and psychological terms, to the

> thoughts so bountiful and wise
> As yours beneath the ever-breaking bough,
> And vast compassion curving like the skies.

Another poem about a special type of persona, "The Bird," demonstrates a technical competence which, in a few ways, equals or surpasses that of

Gerard Manley Hopkins; it has few loose ends, few interruptions of the strict flow of logic:

The Bird

Adventurous bird walking upon the air,
Like a schoolboy running and loitering, leaping and springing,
Pensively pausing, suddenly changing your mind
To turn at ease on the heel of a wing-tip. Where
In all the crystalline world was there to find
For your so delicate walking and airy winging
A floor so perfect, so firm and so fair,
And where a ceiling and walls so sweetly ringing,
Whenever you sing, to your clear singing?

The wide-winged soul itself can ask no more
Than such a pure, resilient and endless floor
For its strong-pinioned plunging and soaring and
        upward and upward springing.[9]

The poem is simple in its basic conception; by dealing in descriptive terms in the first nine lines, the poet prepares for the last three lines, which make their philosophic point using imagery similar to that of the beginning. What Muir asks for is a kind of action of the soul, similar in quality to the action of the bird already described. One notable technical feature of this poem is the use of words ending in -ing, which are ordinarily not good words for poems. This is particularly so when such participles are used in isolation; by the proliferation of -ing words in the text, the author overcomes the aesthetic problem. However, the centrality of the realistic referential value of phases and words such as "walking upon the air," "running and loitering, leaping and springing,/Pensively pausing," "changing your mind," "To turn at ease on the heel of a wing-tip," "delicate walking and airy winging," and, by analogy, "strong-pinioned plunging and soaring and upward and upward springing" is just as important. The picture presented is much more active and modern than in Yeats's "Sailing to Byzantium" where the bird is

set upon a golden bough to sing
To lords and ladies by Byzantium
Of what is past, or passing, or to come.

9. "The Bird," p. 120.

In the poem "Sappho,"[10] Muir deals specifically with the possible problems of tenderness and sensitivity in love insofar as they lead to a tragic
event. What Muir does in essence is to speak of the tendency in Sappho's
life and attitudes which is leading to her destruction. He may be speaking of
something outside of the poetess that is somehow involved in her development—something beyond the circumstances involved in the development
of the tragedy. Muir speaks of the poetess in laudatory terms when he says

>   the found blue trap of day
> (That soon will lock its jail of miseries),

implying that if Sappho, who was noted for sensitivity in her poetry,
had lived longer, then civilization might have profited much more. The
poem can be read in terms of a triangle, with a third person—a woman—
who is somehow involved in Sappho's relationship to Phaon. Strict in its
lack of sentimentality, "Sappho" is typical of many of Muir's poems in that
a sense of tragedy is extended from metaphor to metaphor. Sustaining this
sense of tragedy until the end, the poem closes with the death of the
Greek poet-teacher:

> Now the dumb hulks of being rise around her:
> Beast, rock and tree, illegible figures, stare
> At her in destitution as on the day
> Before the first day broke, when all was nameless,
> Nameless earth, water, firmament, and nameless
> Woman and man. Till on the utmost edge
> She leans above the unanswering shapes of life,
> Cries once and leaps, and battered on the stones,
> Batters love, Phaon and all the misery out.

Muir was correct in assuming that Sappho would be translated later into
modern diction, and that she might subsequently prove to be even more
popular than Catullus with later poets. The picture here created of the
poetess as a sensitive, tragic figure reminds us that life could deal as harshly
with its victims in the past as it can do in the present.

Both "The Rider Victory" and "The Intercepter" are notable for two
qualities: an accomplished use of personification, and the creation of poem
out of an abstraction.

10. "Sappho," p. 131.

The Rider Victory

The rider Victory reins his horse
Midway across the empty bridge
As if head-tall he had met a wall.
Yet there was nothing there at all,
No bodiless barrier, ghostly ridge
To check the charger in his course
So suddenly, you'd think he'd fall.

Suspended, horse and rider stare
Leaping on air and legendary.
In front the waiting kingdom lies,
The bridge and all the roads are free;
But halted in implacable air
Rider and horse with stony eyes
Uprear their motionless statuary.

The Intercepter

Whatever I do, wherever I go,
This is my everlasting care:
The Intercepter haunts my ways
And checks me everywhere.

I leave him at the end of the street
And wander careless through the lands.
Right in the middle of the road
The Intercepter stands.

When dreaming on the dreaming hills,
I let my thoughts roam far and wide,
The Intercepter lifts his hand
And closes up my side.

Asleep, awake, at work or play,
Whatever I do, wherever I go,
The Intercepter bars my way,
And to my 'Yes' says 'No'.

Is he my friend or my enemy,
Betrayer, saviour from disgrace?
The Intercepter frowns at me
With my own frowning face.

Both of these poems jell rhythmically; poems also work through Muir's realization of fine thought and imagery. In "The Rider Victory" a kind of historical fact is examined. By writing about what ought, in some cases, to be a fact, the poet may hope to make slight alterations in contemporary or future history (or our thoughts about the past); thus he offers some hope that the victor may be magnanimous. In spite of the fact that "in front the waiting kingdom lies,"

> Rider and horse with stony eyes
> Uprear their motionless statuary.

In another sense the poem works if we read it in terms of a plea, in so many words, for safety for the conqueror. The poet may be urging future conquerors to proceed with care, to examine the real situation adequately. "The Intercepter" brings to a nightmare level the common enough sense in real life of being thwarted, in both a particular and a general sense. The poem speaks of "whatever I do" in the sense of being thwarted by something with respect to one's deeds and one's actions in relationship to reality; and "wherever I go," refers to the different paths one might follow in life, or, to speak of the same thing, in the "journeys" one might make. The poet extends the intercepter's role to the realm of thoughts and dreams at the beginning of stanza 3, where "thoughts roam far and wide" and are "dreaming on the dreaming hills."

In contrast to this, in another poem, "The Charm,"[11] exploring relationships between men and women, Muir discusses the relationship of Helen to either Paris, an older man, or a hypothetical lover. The "drug that Helen knew" is perhaps symbolic of a woman's wiles, romantic ways, and knowledge of how to charm men. Its effect in the poem is to lessen the sense of guilt on the part of Helen's bemused lovers and admirers.

> There was a drug that Helen knew.
> Dropped in the wine-cup it could take
> All memory and all grief away,
> And while the drinker, wide awake,
> Sat in his chair, indifference grew
> Around him in the estranging day.
> He saw the colours shine and flow,
> The giant lineaments break and change,
> But all storyless, all strange.

11. "The Charm," pp. 218–219.

Here Muir uses Greek personae. One of the best-known myths about
Helen is that of Paris stealing her, or arranging for her to be stolen, and
also the relationship of these events to the fall of Troy. Helen, by possess-
ing the drug, can ease the moral guilt of men with respect to her beauty;
consequently, one is more likely to forgive figures such as Paris, or even
Agamemnon (a suggestion perhaps in the poem). Reading the poem, it is
possible to add the proposition that forgiving an evil action is viable only
insofar as the action is not evil with respect to something else. It does seem
possible to define something as evil in itself, but as not being evil in
relationship to something, or someone else, in a different set of circumstances. Indeed, Muir acknowledges a possible danger:

> So strong the enchantment, Homer says,
> That if this man's own son had died,
> Killed at his feet, his dreaming gaze
> (Like a false-hearted summer day
> Watching the hunter and his prey
> At ease) would not have changed at all,
> Nor his heart knocked against his side.

Then, Muir, as it were, takes up the problem of good and evil in relationship to certain things; the poem closes:

> But far within him something cried
> For the great tragedy to start,
> The pang in lingering mercy fall,
> And sorrow break upon his heart.

The drug is likely to wear off—by itself, but also through the assertion of
something within the person who is drugged. In either case, if something
evil in itself is avoided we are thankful. Man is not free from action in
the realm of tragedy, for "the great tragedy" might start when the drug
wears off. If tragedy is to ensue, then the drug can be seen as having
positive effects. Thus the drug can be seen as morally effective in two
ways. In the first place it may incite evil; in the second, the delaying action
of the drug may prevent a tragedy.

   "Telemachos Remembers,"[12] another of Muir's many poems dealing with
the Greek stories, deals with the specific problems of innocence and
experience, reaching its climax in the last two stanzas after a series of

---

12. "Telemachos Remembers," pp. 219–220.

psychological explorations. Telemachos considers the predicament of his mother, Penelope:

> If she had pushed it to the end,
> Followed the shuttle's cunning song
> So far she had no thought to rend
> In time the web from end to end,
> She would have worked a matchless wrong.
>
> Instead, that jumble of heads and spears,
> Forlorn scraps of her treasure trove,
> I wet them with my childish tears
> Not knowing she wove into her fears
> Pride and fidelity and love.

"Twenty years, every day," in the first stanza juxtaposes two phrases about time and increases the sense of monotony. As the poem develops and moves into the second stanza, we realize we are involved in the description of the basic setting of the poem; the poem is a dramatic monologue spoken by Telemachos. The "heroes" are only "half-finished," and are "sad and mum"; that is, they already have an aura about them that is in line with the slaughter that is to occur. Muir speaks of the horses coming "slowly" as if in natural reaction to their fate; then, in the next line, with the poet using the echo of a simple concept, we find that "Time itself was not so slow." The juxtaposition is excellent; the heroes move slowly, but time itself, carrying the heroes to their death, moves more quickly. One might take the very fact of the suitors to be an indication that men are sometimes drawn to evil situations not necessarily because they lack powers of anticipation, but rather through some self-destructive wish. The repetitions of "The weary loom, the weary loom"; the addition of from "year to year"; and the rhyming of "loom" with "room"—all add to the sense of monotony created in the poem's line of thought, and carry the poem rhythmically to the closing two stanzas, in which Telemachos speaks of his earlier youth when he experienced "that jumble of heads and spears," that he "wet" with childish tears. In other words, a kind of premature impatience on Telemachos' part proved to be faulty in nature; the affections he may have developed for the group of suitors proved to be inadequate or wrong-minded when Odysseus was to return. Penelope's action was different—"she wove into her fears Pride and fidelity and love." It is noteworthy that Muir in this case sticks close to the basic Homeric notion of Penelope's loyalty to Odysseus; the most accepted version of the myth and the personae are quite close to Muir's own version.

In another poem that speaks through personae, "The Young Princes,"
Muir takes up the problem of people born to wealth who are displaced
by the processes of time. We are conscious of the princes as members of a
subdued aristocratic class, perhaps the older western European ruling class.
They have often been supplanted with the rise of general democracy:

The Young Princes

There was a time: we were young princelings then
In artless state, with brows as bright and clear
As morning light on a new morning land.
We gave and took with innocent hands, not knowing
If we were rich or poor, or thinking at all
Of yours or mine; we were newcomers still,
And to have asked the use of that or this,
Its price, commodity, profit would have been
Discourtesy to it and shame to us.
We saw the earth stretched out to us in welcome,
But in our hearts we were the welcomers,
And so were courteous to all that was
In high simplicity and natural pride
To be so hailed and greeted with such glory
(Like absentminded kings who are proffered all
And need not have a penny in their pockets).
And when the elders told the ancestral stories,
Even as they spoke we knew the characters,
The good and bad, the simple and sly, the heroes,
Each in his place, and chance that turns the tale
To grief or joy; we saw and accepted all.
Then in the irreversible noonday came,
Showering its darts into our open breasts,
Doubt that kills courtesy and gratitude
Since then we have led our dull discourteous lives,
Heaven doubting and earth doubting. Earth and heaven
Bent to our menial use. And yet sometimes
We still, as through a dream that comes and goes,
Know what we are, remembering what we were.

The setting of the poem is immediately established in the first line. With
the phrase "we were young princelings then" any doubts about who is
talking are removed. The next cluster of images is one of the two most

imaginative groups in the poems. The poet speaks of "brows" like "morning light," "bright and clear." Giving and taking "with innocent hands," the young princes were newcomers. The next section offers a fine example of language that is concrete as well as general. In their former state of existence the princes were "welcomers" and "courteous to all," "hailed and greeted" in a state of "high simplicity and natural pride." As if to avoid charges of Georgian pomposity, Muir is careful to switch to a sequence of ideas pertaining to education about, and knowledge of, traditional reality. Then, as in a sonnet, and as expectantly as one might reach the end of a sonnet (Muir has made it clear that the princes are speaking of a past time) we become aware of the present, which contrasts quite sharply with the past. Muir closes with the suggestion that "remembrance of things past" has some value as something enjoyable in a reduced present. There can be no doubt that Muir wrote this poem as an acknowledgement that there is no substitute for a condition of total and general wealth in a society for everyone. If wealth is achievable for only a few, it should remain in the correct hands. Muir, like most sensible people, knows that wealth breeds things far better than and far beyond mere happiness.

Thus, we see that Edwin Muir uses specific personae in a number of ways. In the "Ballad of Hector in Hades," "The Charm," and "Telemachos Remembers" he created significant variations on Homeric myths, modifying them slightly or adding an element of psychological realism. In poems like "Then," "The Intercepter," and "The Rider Victory" Muir made use of unusual ideas from anthropology and comparative politics that take on strength and originality in his hands. By choosing fresh and unique subject matter the poet extended both the frontiers of modern world poetry and also improved our understanding of what a persona in a poem can consist of. Poems such as "The Young Princes," "Merlin," "The Little General," and "The Old Gods" deal with literary characters that one might be likely to ignore against the background of twentieth-century poetry, and the ideas out of which the poems spring could be seen as stemming from older literatures and traditions. "Then" reminds the student of modern poetry that even the most archaic, simple processes (usually a fit subject for science) can take on life in the poet's hands. A poem like "The Bird" reminds us that even the most shopworn subject matter can live a little in the hands of a master poet. Whether dealing with villains, gods, déclassé aristocrats, or animals—or simply adding personification or characterization to ideas—the poet looks at his subjects with appropriate language and attitudes, and with enough skill and craftsmanship to put all the elements and ingredients together into poetry.

VI

Place Poems, Franz Kafka, and "The Transfiguration"

The significance of Muir's poetry taken as a whole can cover a wider area if we examine what might be called "Place poems" (if one can borrow from the book titles *Journeys and Places*[1] and *The Narrow Place*,[2] as well as titles of ten of the poems: "The Unfamiliar Plaçe,"[3] "The Place of Light and Darkness,"[4] "The Solitary Place,"[5] "The Private Place,"[6] "The Unattained Place,"[7] "The Threefold Place,"[8] "The Original Place,"[9] "The Sufficient Place,"[10] "The Dreamt-of Place,"[11] and "The Narrow Place"[12]). If one thinks of Muir in these poems, as it were, building his own system to live with in the face of a modern universe believed by many to be unpopulated by gods, rulers, or systems, one would not be too far off. The poems are rather like a Catholic mass: inexplicable yet noteworthy, and, in some cases, bene-

1. Muir, E., *Journeys and Places* (London: Dent, 1937).

2. Muir, E., *The Narrow Place* (London: Faber, 1943).

3. "The Unfamiliar Place," pp. 78–79.

4. "The Place of Light and Darkness," pp. 79–80.

5. "The Solitary Place," pp. 80–81.

6. "The Private Place," p. 82.

7. "The Unattained Place," pp. 83–84.

8. "The Threefold Place," p. 85.

9. "The Original Place," pp. 85–86.

10. "The Sufficient Place," pp. 86–87.

11. "The Dreamt-of Place," pp. 87–88.

12. "The Narrow Place," pp. 101–102.

ficial. Insofar as they can be thought of as musical pieces, they constitute, as it were, a modern hymnology; but thinking of these poems simply as poems takes us close enough to mythology and metaphysics.

One might think of this century as one where, by and large, the individual has come to the fore, and the dominant organization of society has been based on the fulfillment of each person as a single unit. With the evolution from state to church to individual, the poet—with his single, lyrical voice—can provide what state and church may no longer provide: an individual ethos. The *Odyssey* served the purposes of the Greek city federation; the Bible provided guidance for a thousand years of religious domination. With writers like Chaucer, Montaigne, and Shakespeare, the individual took on weight in the social structure. Milton worked in terms of the Protestant ethic, which was generally more concerned with the individual's freedom of decision than traditional Catholicism was. In the twentieth century, the individual becomes more and more prevalent; and in poets like Edwin Muir the individual's thought and action take on metaphysical, religious, and mythological dimensions in themselves. The place poems are good examples of the modern, individualistic dimensions of metaphor. By applying techniques of practical criticism we may see where the poet has gone; and the analogies we have found with the work of Franz Kafka let us see Muir more clearly in relationship to a near contemporary.

In "The Unfamiliar Place" the use of the word "place" in both the title and the first line ("I do not know this place,") introduces the theme and serves as an echo or thread that one has to keep in mind when interpreting the ensuing verse structures centered on the concept of place. It would appear as if the poet wishes us to remember a kind of physical presence in a particular unfamiliar place as part of the occasion of the poem. In spite of a long time on earth the poet is not familiar with where he has come in his "changing race." The image of the moon suggests the dark side of life; that of the sun suggests just the opposite. With a lack of modesty often characteristic of poets, the poet sees himself in the same realm as "Christ and Caesar," and also "the first man." Like many historical men, Muir is "far up the mountainside" and in a condition, no doubt, above that of the average individual.

Muir must mean by "this turning light" something similar to Wordsworth's intimations of immortality, except that what is being talked about is more appropriately summed up in expressions like "absolute truth," "metaphysical coherence," or "mystical apprehension of God." The poet implies that such consciousness has been omnipresent with him always and at all times. Applying the story, from the Christian Bible of the Garden Of Eden and the Fall, the poet states the nature of his quest:

> In the unnumbered names
> My fathers gave these things
> I seek a kingdom lost,

The poet thus becomes a name-giver in the most fundamental sense: he is in the region of what some philosophers call "truth," and at the same time in history. The language at the end of the stanza switches to that of the subconscious and, lastly, that of the mystic:

> I have questioned many a ghost
> Far inland in my dreams,
> Enquired of fears and shames
> The dark and winding way
> To the day within my day.

The use of "ghost" implies that there are serious apprehensions on the part of the poet about everyday reality—and "my dreams" coupled with "questioned" suggests that the imagery and ideas of dreams may have more than merely physically suggestive significance.

In stanza 3, Muir proceeds to a series of divisions or distinctions, and implies that such visions of reality have a certain value in spite of what may be described as bewilderment. A further implication is that being alert with respect to one's perceptions involves a condition superior to that of sensual or intellectual torpor.

> And aloft I have stood
> And given my eyes their fill,
> Have watched the bad and the good
> Go up and down the hill,
> The peasants on the plain
> Ploughing the fields red,
> The roads running alone,
> The ambush in the wood,
> The victim walking on,
> The misery-blackened door
> That never will open again,
> The tumblers at the fair,
> The watchers on the stair,
> Cradle and bridal-bed,
> The living and the dead
> Scattered on every shore.

The poet has seen good men and bad ones; he has seen men who were in a state of utmost simplicity; he has seen those who take life and those who are victims; he has seen those made bitter; he has seen those dwelling in a state of comic relief from life's harshness; he has observed those too highly introspective or too highly intelligent or sensitive for their own good; lastly, he has seen many born and many who spend their time in sexual bondage. Summing up, the poet acknowledges that something more final, more truthful in nature awaits in spite of all experience:

> But I am balked by fear
> And what my lips say
> To drown the voice of fear.
> The earthly day waits.

"The Place of Light and Darkness" sums up the way an individual—a farmer or a husbandman—might think about his experience. A field is indeed a place of light and darkness, insofar as it is used in the summer, and, for the most part, lies dormant in the winter. Thinking in terms of a wheat harvest is perhaps more appropriate in that, in the old processes, after wheat was cut, it was left standing for about six hours before it was gathered—so that harvesting made the day extend into the night. In the first seven lines the experience is depicted in a mood similar to that of the earlier "Childhood:"[13]

> Walking on the harvest hills of Night
> Time's elder brother, the great husbandman,
> Goes on his ancient round. His massive lantern,
> Simpler than the first fashion, lights the rows
> Of stooks that lean like little golden graves
> Or tasselled barges foundering low
> In the black stream.

In the dark the farmer is reminded of the summer, "day all yellow and red, flowers, fruit, and corn," "soft hair harvest-golden," "children playing," and

> The lover standing by the trysting-tree
> Who'll never find his love till all are gathered
> In light or darkness.

13. "Childhood," p. 19.

As if being reminded of former good conditions that were not enough, the reverie is broken:

> A wind shakes
> The loaded sheaves, the feathery tomb bursts open,
> And yellow hair is poured along the ground
> From the bent neck of time. The woods cry:
> *This is the resurrection.*

Like most people the farmer's life is characterized by work and by certain central events. In the case of the poem we meet a man at work who engages in introspection with respect to his life. An accident suggests a kind of "little judgment day" in that the farmer may have been ignoring the task at hand by daydreaming, or else—and it remains unspecified—a kind of divine justice or chance event has been operating due to some aberration in the past. Yet

> He goes on,
> Bearing within his ocean-heart the jewel,
> The day all yellow and red wherein a sun
> Shines on the endless harvest lands of time.

The farmer has taken the life of the wheat, as it were, and the process of growth for the year is virtually finished. Yet within are the memory and the vision of how to bring life to the earth, how to treat living things. Errors made in the past may be avoided during the next year and harvest. Late summer and its glories will return. In a way the poems operate on two levels: first, the farmer, "the great husbandman," moves from the "light" and life of late summer to the "darkness" of the winter; and second, the "light" of the central events in life gives way to the "darkness" of hard work. Whatever Muir's intent may be, he has evoked a picture of the country that is reminiscent of Thomas Hardy in novel after novel. Muir reminds us that the basic business of gathering food of some sort, in some form, is central for most endeavor.

"The Solitary Place" raises the point of human loneliness and insufficiency against the background of immortality. It is fundamentally an unhappy poem, although its attitudes toward death and life may be described as shifting:

> O I shall miss
> With one small breath these centuries

> Of harvest-home uncounted!
> I have known
> The mead, the bread,
> And the mounds of grain
> As half my riches. But the fields will change,
> And their harvest would be strange
> If I could return. I should know again
> Only the lint-white stubble plain
> From which the summer-painted birds have flown
> A year's life on.

In the first three lines of the poem Muir discusses what would be his attitude toward life or reality after he should die, or if in life he should completely absent himself from the experience of reality. Nature, manufactured goods, and abundance have been known as half of life by the poet in the midst of things. If he should return after death, or after a period of withdrawal, the poet would be puzzled by changes, and what he would find would be stark in its newness and inadequate.

We may have been led by the poet's speculations to believe that we might be in the presence of someone whose insight penetrated the mysteries of life and death; but the second stanza disproves this assumption:

> But I can never
> See with these eyes the double-threaded river
> That runs through life and death and death and life,
> Weaving one scene.

The modesty of the poet here appears to be similar to the modesty of most serious people with respect to our most fundamental assumptions. The poet goes on:

> Which I and not I
> Blindfold have crossed, I and not I
> Will cross again, my face, my feet, my hands
> Gleaned from lost lands
> To be sown again.

An analogy is drawn between the processes of life and death, and the processes of sharing or not sharing in life itself. "Lost lands" implies a kind of region or area where one has been even in introspective reverie, or in physical absence from earth itself; the images imply multiple areas of existence.

Summoning up imagery that calls to mind the Christian Bible and Greek tragedy, the poet calls to mind the fables or myths that inform racial history, with respect to both their metaphorical relevance and their truth to historical fact:

> O certain prophecy,
> And faithful tragedy,
> Furnished with scenery of sorrow and strife,
> The Cross and the Flood
> And Babel's towers
> And Abel's blood
> And Eden's bowers,
> Where I and not I
> Lived and questioned and made reply:
> None else to ask or make reply...

In stanza 2 the poet may be thought of as having, as it were, commented upon his own relevance as a prophet—a function that is traditionally a part of the poetic life. The word "prophecy" holds strength in stanza 3, insofar as the past prophecies of man were essentially tragic or problematical. "Certain prophecy" suggests, in terms of life, that life often seems determined from without, and in terms of fiction, that events predicted in the Christian Bible have a way of working themselves out eventually on the stage of life. The lines "faithful tragedy/Furnished with scenery of sorrow and strife" suggest the early visions of Aeschylus and Sophocles. "Cross" of course summons up the unhappy fate of Jesus in the world. The "Flood" calls up the story of Noah and the role of fate, or God, in predetermining "tragedy" for life. "Babel's towers" suggests human cross purposes. "Abel's blood" suggests the possibility and reality of violence even between members of the human race. "Eden's bowers" suggests that, in spite of conditions of "paradise in life," there are darker "bowers"; it also recalls the principal story of man's permanent expulsion (largely self-induced) from a better life. One might also regard the first two lines of this third stanza as simply holding some referential relevance to life and death themselves: the "certain prophecy" is the life of man in time, from birth onward; the "faithful tragedy" is the reality of death that faces everyone.

The last three lines of stanza 3 have served as an introduction to the fourth and last stanza by presenting some elemental questions or paradoxes. There is always an "I" and always a "not I": the self is autonomous and individual, yet at the same time compounded of something else. The self "lived," "questioned," and assumed some answers ("made reply"): yet the

self was basically alone and there was "none else to ask or make reply."
Muir then uses a modern scientific idea (the apparatus of human vision)
coupled with the old philosophical idea of reality as being in the eye of the
beholder to make a poem called "The Solitary Place" even more problematical. It is the reality and validity of "something else" that are called into
doubt by stanza 4:

> If there is none else to ask or reply
> But I and not I,
> And when I stretch out my hand my hand comes towards me
> To pull me across to me and back to me,
> If my own mind, questioning, answers me
> And there is no other answer to me,
> If all that I see,
> Woman and man and beast and rock and sky,
> Is a flat image shut behind an eye,
> And only my thoughts can meet me or pass me or follow me,
> O then I am alone,
> I, many and many in one,
> A lost player upon a hill
> On a sad evening when the world is still,
> The house empty, brother and sister gone
> Beyond the reach of sight, or sound of any cry,
> Into the bastion of the mind, behind the shutter of the eye.

Thus not only material realities, but the nature of life after death, history,
and the nature of the self and other humans are all seen as being subject to
questions.

A problem of individuality takes on new dimensions in "The Private
Place," but in contrast to "The Solitary Place," the considerations of individuality are likely to effect more significant action in that the poem is couched
in dual terms: those of the existing self and the other. In contrast to "The
Solitary Place," "The Private Place" accepts a priori the existence of the self
and the other:

> This stranger holding me from head to toe,
> This deaf usurper I shall never know,
> Who lives in household quiet in my unrest,
> And of my troubles weaves his tranquil nest,
> Who never smiles or frowns or bows his head,
> And while I rage is insolent as the dead,

> Composed, indifferent, thankless, faithful, he
> Is my ally and only enemy.

This stanza develops a kind of negative alter ego to go along with the self. There is a "deaf usurper" who cannot be recognized, one who "lives in household quiet" and "weaves his tranquil nest" despite the poet's malaise. The "usurper" "never smiles or frowns or bows his head," and while the poet rages "is insolent as the dead, Composed, indifferent, thankless, faithful." He is, ironically, the poet's "ally and only enemy" at the same time and much for the worse.

In contrast to this condition the poet then develops a metaphor expressive of "the other," another person, and sharing:

> Come then, take up the cleansing blade once more
> That drives all difference out. The fabled shore
> Sees us again. Now the predestined fight,
> The ancestral stroke, the opening gash of light;
> Side by side myself by myself slain,
> The wakening stir, the eyes loaded with gain
> Of ocean darkness, the rising hand in hand,
> I with myself at one, the changed land,
> My home, my country.

The "cleansing blade" is that which strikes down barriers between the poet and other people and establishes points of human commonness; these contacts are spoken of as "the fabled shore." The poet uses imagery reminiscent of the story of the flight from Eden, the legend of Abel and Cain, and the aftermath of these events with the proliferation of the human race. But the flight from Eden is "predestined," the "stroke" is that of the brothers' partial reconciliation, and the "gash of light" involves growth in time from the early tragic events of man's history. Consequently Muir transmutes the stories of creation and origin to lighten the burden of moral guilt, in this case to forward the cause of the poet reaching out toward the other— the condition wherein we find "the wakening stir," "eyes loaded with gain," "the rising hand in hand," the "I with myself at one," "the changed land," the "home," the "country," and the "boundless treasure." However, this condition gives way in the poem to the "deaf usurper" again. Finally, the poet admits:

> I hold this life
> Only in strife and the aftertaste of strife

With this dull champion and thick-witted king.
But at one word he'll leap into the ring.

"The Unattained Place" operates in the realm of highly suggestive images that are probably meant to call up two areas of experience: good deeds and ambitions.

We have seen the world of good deeds spread
With its own sky above it
A length away
Our whole day,
Yet have not crossed from our false kindred.
We could have leapt straight from the womb to bliss
And never lost it after,
Been cradled, baptized, bred in that which is
And never known this frontier laughter,
But that we hate this place so much
And hating love it,
And that our weakness is such
That it must clutch
All weakness to it and can never release
The bound and battling hands,
The one hand bound, the other fighting
The fellow-foe it's tied to, righting
Weakness with weakness, rending, reuniting
The torn and incorruptible bands
That bind all these united and disunited lands,—
While there lies our predestined power and ease,
There, in those natural fields, life-fostering seas.

In mentioning the "world of good deeds'" early the poet establishes the theme that most of the rest of the poem is related to. With the statement about "false kindred" and what follows the poet implies that man operates for the most part in a realm of ambition with victories and acquisitions as the empty result. Not only that, but most of us have a touch of the Zarathustran overreacher in us, insofar as we are related to what Muir calls the "frontier." If we think strictly in terms of "that which is," and the stanza in which it occurs, it, as it were, joins "that which is" with "the world of good deeds." What is referred to next is the "Unattained Place"—that place where we have not been, that ideal not obtained, that lover not yet gathered. We "hate this place so much" that we "love it"; in other words, whether we are speaking of the world of good deeds or those things unattained, a kind of spiritual work is required to overcome the instinct of hate. Even then we encounter

> The bound and battling hands,
> The one hand bound, the other fighting
> The fellow-foe it's tied to.

If life is a battle, then we can see the world of good deeds spread before us as an alternative to the busy, everyday selfish actions of most men, or the men who search after truth so much that they ignore too readily the stances of the saint, of the savior, or even of simple and moving men of good will.

The poet then asks if we could somehow divorce ourself from the realm of past action—of normal selfish action. Even if we could do so, paradoxically, we would also be removing the good things out of which we sprang—most notably the positive, innocent events of childhood. These childish states are accepted by the poet as being closest to "the realm of good deeds"; yet at the same time, again paradoxically, these same grounds contain the seeds of overreaching. And, in a sense, the poet establishes still another paradox in his closing line:

> Yet from that missing heaven outspread
> Here all we read.

Present life is seen as being connected with dreams of youth; one has to have been alive, it would appear, in order to sense "the world of good deeds spread" before the experiences. We can think of "the world of good deeds" as coexistent with the "Unattained Place," and the same thing—in that action in terms of goodness often results in evil consequences. Therefore, mere "good deeds" are not enough; in fact, they often seem unattainable in the light of negative consequences.

"The Threefold Place" deals with the problem of violence, principally depicting what is the normal condition both before and after the violent events. Unlike Homer in the *Iliad* and the *Odyssey*, or Virgil in the *Aeneid*, Muir spends little time with descriptions of battles, but instead, in the first four lines, draws up a physical description of the setting and evokes an atmosphere. Then in the following four lines the battle actually takes place:

> Soon

> Out of the russet woods in amber mail

> Heroes come walking through the yellow sheaves,
> Walk on and meet. And then a silent gale
> Scatters them on the field like autumn leaves.

Then in imagery similar to the first four lines (similar to the "birds," the meadow imagery, and the silence) the poet swiftly describes the aftermath. However, it is in the last five lines that the poem acquires genuine distinction:

> One field. I look again and there are three:
>   One where the heroes fell to rest,
> One where birds make of iron limbs a tree,
>   Helms for a nest,
> And one where grain stands up like armies drest.

One might think in political terms: of the right, the center, and the left, successively. However, it is more important to think of progressions. As we think of the place "where the heroes fell to rest" we think (perhaps unfortunately) in terms of a shrine, and therefore a place of history—a place where something has already been "worked out." The horror is something in the past. As for the birds making "of iron limbs a tree," we are reminded of continuation beyond the events of the battle. A kind of historical artifice has been created that is somewhat different than it was before changes had been made. The "grain" suggests the continuation and growth of life itself beyond mere mechanical contrivance. And then, moving beyond a facile optimism and thinking in cyclical terms, the poet reminds us that the "grain stands up like armies drest."

By using italics in two stanzas of the four of "The Original Place" the poet reminds us that within a single poem different voices may be used in contradiction. Our attitude toward "The Original Place" may vary with respect to which stanzas we read. The optimistic stanzas are noteworthy with respect to the clarity they achieve as well as the way they suggest many things at the same time, and the two pessimistic passages are almost equally intricate:

> *This is your native land.*
> *By ancient inheritance*
> *Your lives are free, though a hand*
> *Strange to you set you here,*
> *Ordained this liberty*
> *And gave you hope and fear*
> *And the turning maze of chance.*

To weave our tale of Time
Rhyme is knit to rhyme
So close, it's like a proof
That nothing else can be
But this one tapestry
Where gleams under the woof
A giant Fate half-grown,
Imprisoned and its own.

To your unquestioned rule
No bound is set. You were
Made for this work alone.
This is your native air.
You could not leave these fields.
And when Time is grown
Beneath your countless hands
They say this kingdom shall
Be stable and beautiful.

But at its centre stands
A stronghold never taken,
Stormed at hourly in vain,
Held by a force unknown
That neither answers nor yields.
There our arms are shaken,
There the hero was slain
That bleeds upon our shields.

In the first and more pessimistic passage the fact that things are so close
(as evidenced in daily contact and, particularly, strong feelings about each
other) is suggestive that humans might be the only form of life, and unique.
However, we are only "half-grown," "imprisoned," and lonely in our
singularity. In the second negative stanza we come up against that which
we cannot be, or the unattainable—that which we call universal, absolute,
and the truth.

"The Sufficient Place," one of Muir's best poems, could very well have
been discussed as a love poem. In all these earlier poems of place we have,
as it were, been dealing with problematical or even tragic aspects of
existence. Even in "The Original Place"—a kind of substitute poem for the
myth of Eden, man's Fall, and his expulsion from paradise—ended with
"the hero" that "was slain/That bleeds upon our shields." However, "The
Sufficient Place" moves squarely and rather happily to "Man and Woman,"
the home, and the fact that "This is the Pattern, these the Archetypes":

The Sufficient Place

See, all the silver roads wind in, lead in
To this still place like evening. See, they come
Like messengers bearing gifts to this little house,
And this great hill worn down to a patient mound,
And these tall trees whose motionless branches bear
An aeon's summer foliage, leaves so thick
They seem to have robbed a world of shade, and kept
No room for all these birds that line the boughs
With heavier riches, leaf and bird and leaf.
Within the doorway stand
Two figures, Man and Woman, simple and clear
As a child's first images. Their manners are
Such as were known before the earliest fashion
Taught the Heavens guile. The room inside is like
A thought that needed thus much space to write on,
Thus much, no more. Here all's sufficient. None
That comes complains, and all the world comes here,
Comes, and goes out again, and comes again.
This is the Pattern, these the Archetypes,
Sufficient, strong, and peaceful. All outside
From end to end of the world is tumult. Yet
These roads do not turn in here but writhe on
Round the wild earth for ever. If a man
Should chance to find this place three times in time
His eyes are changed and make a summer silence
Amid the tumult, seeing the roads wind in
To their still home, the house and the leaves and birds.

Using the imagery of roads to start the poem, Muir couples the concepts of "sufficient place" and "still place" to give some idea of, but not give away, what he regards as sufficient. The image of "bearing gifts" reminds us that truly happy people—such as the "Man and Woman" here—may find the world full of "gifts," of opportunities for further happiness; for a unique spirit of benevolence often operates instinctively in the presence of the happily married. The "great hill worn down to a patient mound" suggests both the forces (often other people's attitudes) that marriage is subjected to and what is often the best response—patience. The "tall trees" bespeak a kind of nobility which is more that of emotional adequacy than of birth, as well as the instinctive forces surrounding or involved in marriage. It often seems as if the world is laid out for lovers:

> Here all's sufficient. None
> That comes complains, and all the world comes here,

In lines 10 through 20, the poet uses language magnificently to express the inexpressible. But lines 23 through 27 seem somewhat puzzling:

> If a man
> Should chance to find this place three times in time

"The Dreamt-of Place" approaches the problem of the relation of life to human loyalty in love; for a total loyalty between two lovers is indeed impossible according to the most ultimate standards of psychology and spirit. No matter how loyal one might be with one's body, an instinctive force impels one toward someone else at times. According to ultimate moral standards, these might be regarded as blasphemies; in terms of life, it would appear, they are problems likely to occur. This type of problem is what Muir approaches in this poem—particularly in the title, which is just about, but not quite, ironic:

The Dreamt-of Place

> I saw two towering birds cleaving the air
> And thought they were Paolo and Francesca
> Leading the lost, whose wings like silver billows
> Rippled the azure sky from shore to shore,
> They were so many. The nightmare god was gone
> Who roofed their pain, the ghastly glen lay open,
> The hissing lake was still, the fiends were fled,
> And only some few headless, footless mists
> Crawled out and in the iron-hearted caves.
> Like light's unearthly eyes the lost looked down,
> And heaven was filled and moving. Every height
> On earth was thronged and all that lived stared upward.
> I thought, This is the reconciliation,
> This is the day after the Last Day,
> The lost world lies dreaming within its coils,
> Grass grows upon the surly sides of Hell,
> Time has caught time and holds it fast for ever.
> And then I thought, Where is the knife, the butcher,
> The victim? Are they all here in their places?
> Hid in this harmony? But there was no answer.

The Paolo and Francesca episode in the *Inferno* is perhaps the most famous case of adultery. By using a case of physical aberration as an example and describing "what is not," the poet evokes "The Dreamt-of Place"—a world without small or large adulterous actions. It is a world divorced from Dante's hell. Everything is good and right, and all problems are solved. Christ might have asked early in relation to planning his own course of actions the same questions that Muir does:

> Where is the knife, the butcher,
> The victim? Are they all here in their places?
> Hid in this harmony?

Obviously the scene is threatened. Muir's last place poem, "The Narrow Place," comes perhaps inappropriately last. Although it is a deep statement of reconciliation, at the same time it involves acceptance of what one might call "limited area." This latter fact might suggest that Muir achieved "limited area" when in point of fact this is not the case.

Muir's first published translation of Kafka in book form was *The Castle*,[14] which appeared in Great Britain in March, 1930—just five years after Muir's own first book of poems, *First Poems*,[15] came out; four years after *Chorus of the Newly Dead*;[16] two years before *Six Poems*;[17] and four years before *Variations on a Time Theme*;[18] was to appear. From 1930 to 1948, in point of fact, there were to be six volumes of Kafka in Great Britain: *The Castle*; *The Great Wall of China, and Other Pieces*[19] in 1933; *The Trial*[20] in 1937; *America*[21] in 1938; *Parables, in German and*

14. Franz Kafka, *The Castle* (London: Secker, 1930).

15. *First Poems* (London: Hogarth, 1925).

16. *Chorus of the Newly Dead* (London: Hogarth, 1926).

17. *Six Poems* (Warlingham: Samson, 1932).

18. *Variations on a Time Theme* (London: Dent, 1934).

19. Franz Kafka, *The Great Wall of China, and Other Pieces* (London: Secker, 1933).

20. Franz Kafka, *The Trial* (London: Secker, 1937).

21. Franz Kafka, *America* (London: Routledge, 1938).

English[22] in 1947; and *In the Penal Settlement: Tales and Short Pieces*[23] in 1948. Because the translations required a great deal of attention, and because most of the "Place Poems" seem to stem out of the years prior to 1937, it is not inappropriate to mention the two threads of Muir's literary career in relation to each other.

On October 31, 1935, in the *New English Weekly*,[24] Edwin Muir provided his readers with an apt comparison of Dostoevsky, Dickens, Joyce, D. H. Lawrence, and Kafka in terms of the way these artists ended their novels. The uniqueness of Dickens, according to Muir, lies in comparison with those before, who "had been generally content to leave his heroes with a fortune and married happiness." Dickens, instead, "provided his characters with a new scale of income":

> Dickens has at least the justification that we can imagine the lives of his characters after he has comfortably settled them, little as we may believe in the settlement: for they do not radically change just at the point where we take leave of them.

In spite of Dostoevsky's brilliance and mastery, he

> leaves his characters hanging in the air with their hearts changed; he assumes that after that everything is well; and though that is true in one sense, if we are to accept the facts of religious experience, it is as certainly not true in another, for after the change of heart, if it is sincere, they are bound to have a more severe struggle than before it.

As for D. H. Lawrence:

> At the end of *Sons and Lovers*, Paul walks back to the lights of the town with his head high and his hands clenched, obviously intending to do something vague but unprecedented. Coming where it does, at the end of a story, the act takes on an importance which the reader is of course incapable of measuring. But the suggestion seems to be that Paul is entering on a way of life which is quite different from his former life and quite different also from any life known before by human beings.

Muir included the cosmopolitan Irishman, as well:

22. Franz Kafka, *Parables, in German and English* (New York: Schocken, 1947).

23. Franz Kafka, *In the Penal Settlement: Tales and Short Pieces* (London: Secker, 1948).

24. "Views and Reviews," *New English Weekly* 8 (31 October 1935), pp. 50–51.

At the end of A *Portrait of the Artist as a Young Man*
Stephen Dedalus sets out to forge "the uncreated conscience of
my race," which was something hitherto unattempted.

In contrast with these writers, Muir mentions essential themes of Kafka:

> An antidote to this way of ending the novel may perhaps be
> found in the work of Franz Kafka, who did not end his novels at
> all. His problem was like Dostoevsky's, the problem of salvation,
> but he treated it allegorically, which in his case meant dialec-
> tically, and he saw it as an endless process, or at least a process
> which could not find its end in early experience: the gradual but
> infinitely incomplete approximation of imperfection to perfection...
> A more comprehensive way of putting the same thing would
> be to say that while most of us have discarded the solutions of
> religion and the greater part of the knowledge that went with
> them, the problems of religion still exist within us, asking for
> some answer. The result is a state for which not we but history
> is primarily responsible. The happy ending of the serious modern
> novel is the ideal expression of that state, and Kafka is the only
> modern writer, it seems to me, who has dealt seriously and
> exhaustively with it in imaginative terms. That is one of the
> reasons why he is so important.

The "place poems" of Edwin Muir grow out of much the same spirit as
Kafka's novels. In both cases there are heroes. Muir's drama stems out of
the nature of his own explorations of reality in a language that is elemental,
sparse, metaphysical, and mythological. But perhaps it is more appropriate
to speak of "the voice" of Muir's poetry. Rather than dealing with incidents
or realities in terms of incident and development of plot, Muir tries to plot
the way in traditional language of the metaphysical poet—as in the poem
"The Narrow Place:"

> The cloud has drawn so close,
> This small much-trodden mound
> Must, must be very high
> And no road goes by.
> The parsimonious ground
> That at its best will bear
> A few thin blades as fine as hair
> Can anywhere be found,
> Yet is so proud and niggardly
> And envious, it will trust

> Only one little wild half-leafless tree
> To straggle from the dust.

Like the setting of Kafka's novels, the setting or place described as the
scene of the action is both well defined and at the same time not well
defined—thus increasing the aura of mystery. The "places" of Muir's "place
poems" are like Kafka's settings, also, insofar as what we are reminded of is
both daily reality and the world of dreams. Almost every event, every
image (in Muir's case perhaps more so), seems to carry weight beyond
itself. In fact, both Muir and Kafka seem more symbolistic than the French
poets of the nineteenth century who are called Symbolists.

The sometimes neglected "Variations on a Time Theme" (a poem written
after T. S. Eliot's *The Waste Land* and before most of the *Four Quartets*)
can be seen as carrying the same type of surreal, symbolic weight—a
weight that is religious, as distinct from being seen in terms of human
psychological processes:

> There is a stream
> We have been told of. Where it is
> We do not know. But it is not a dream,
> Though like a dream. We cannot miss
> The road that leads us to it. Fate
> Will take us there that keeps us here.
> Neither hope nor fear
> Can hasten or retard the date
> Of our deliverance; when we shall leave this sand
> And enter the unknown and feared and longed-for land.[25]

Truth or the Ultimate, as in Kafka, is conceived of in towerlike imagery.
And, as in much of Kafka, the sense of death is not completely absent and
forms part of the matrix of themes.

If, by not ending his novels, Kafka was true to the modern sense of
religious mystery and of inadequacy with respect to practical religious life,
then Muir and Kafka are similar in this respect. One might argue that
there is resolution in poems like "The Confirmation"[26] and "The Sufficient
Place." Yet these poems contain the seeds of problems and contradictions
in themselves (how does one find the "right one"? or, in the case of "The

25. "Variations on a Time Theme," p. 47.

26. "The Confirmation," p. 118.

Sufficient Place," how does one relate to outer reality?). The whole body of poetic work contains statements about the perennial problems of religion and how salvation may be achieved. Muir could very well have been talking about himself when he spoke of Kafka's lack of ending as indicative of a high degree of unsentimental spiritual malaise. According to Willa Muir, among Edwin Muir's words as he approached death were "There are no absolutes."[27] And as we can see from the examination of the "place poems," the religious "problems" with Muir took on wide dimensions. Whereas we have the feeling that Kafka's young men are, as it were, looking for the path, Muir, in his middle poetry, seems a reflective, more middle-aged pilgrim well on the way. Such religious concern and bewilderment were -finally to drive Muir toward creating a religious figure in his last poem. Here he came very close to what we might call the creation of a savior.

In spite of implications of the particular image or scene in Franz Kafka (such as the insect in "The Metamorphosis"), Muir sees the writer's reasoning as grounded in a more fundamental way of looking at things. For Muir,

Kafka starts with a general or universal situation, not a particular one. This being so, it does not matter where he begins his story, for the situation is always there, and always the same.[28]

Also,

As the situation is universal and stationary, it is also storyless; and this is the point at which Kafka's art begins. He is a great story-teller because there is no story for him to tell; so that he has to make it up. No foundation in fact, no narrative framework, no plot or scene for a plot is there to help him; he has to create the story, character, setting and action, and embody in it his meaning.[29]

Perhaps most accurately,

His stories generally begin in the midway of life, at a point decided by the chance of the moment, and yet at a decisive point, since in the universal situation every point is decisive. The

27. Willa Muir, *Belonging* (London: Hogarth, 1968), p. 315.

28. *Essays on Literature and Society* (Boston: Harvard University Press, 1965). p. 120.

29. Ibid.

image of a road comes into our minds when we think of his
stories; for in spite of all the confusions and contradictions in
which he was involved he held that life was a way, not a chaos,
that the right way exists and can be found by a supreme and
exhausting effort, and that whatever happens every human
being in fact follows some way, right or wrong. The road then is
there; we may imagine beside it a wayside inn from which an
anonymous figure is just emerging. He looks ahead and sees,
perhaps on a distant hill, a shape which he has often seen before
in his journey, but always far away, and apparently inaccessible;
that shape is justice, grace, truth, final reconciliation, father, God.
As he gazes at it he wonders whether he is moving towards it
while it is receding from him, or flying from it while it is
pursuing him. He is tormented by this question, for it is insoluble
by human reasoning. He feels irresistibly drawn towards that
distant shape, and yet cannot overcome his dread of it. Kafka
describes in *The Castle* the struggle to reach it, and in *The Trial*
the flight from it. But the hero can neither reach it nor escape it,
for it is enveloped in a mystery different from the ordinary
mystery of human life, and he does not know the law of that
mystery. The roads leading towards it are therefore deceitful; the
right turn may easily chance to be the wrong, and the wrong the
right.[30]

Some further comments about patterns in Kafka's characters add to our
understanding Muir's view of the novelist:

The frustration of the hero is an intrinsic part of Kafka's
theme; and it is caused by what in theological language is known
as the irreconcilability of the divine and the human law; a subtle
yet immeasurable disparity.[31]

A craftsman himself, Muir comments on Kafka as a craftsman—as an artist
and a master of incident:

He is a great storyteller both by his art and by the interest and
value of what he says. And the value of what he says does not
depend on the truth of his metaphysical structure, any more than
the value of what Dante says depends on his theology. We can

30. Ibid., p. 121.

31. Ibid., p. 122.

read *The Castle* and *The Trial* rejecting his theory of the irreconcilability of divine and human law, and yet find in them the most enchanting discoveries, the most startling riddles, the most profound insights into human life.[32]

For Muir, Kafka's "heroes" are broadly representative in a rather unique way:

> The hero of the two great stories is anybody, and his story is the story of anybody. 'Anybody' is obviously an allegorical figure, fit to be designated as K. or Josef K., as Kafka names the heroes of *The Castle* and *The Trial*. Yet these stories are not allegories. The truths they bring out are surprising or startling, not conventional and expected, as the truths of allegory tend to be. They are more like serious fantasies; the spontaneous expression of Kafka's genius was fantasy, as his early short stories show. Fantasy came as naturally to him as writing. In *The Castle* and *The Trial* he employs it for purposes as serious as any writer has ever attempted. But no designation of his art is satisfying. We can see what it was not; to find a name for it is of little consequence.[33]

If we apply these comments to Muir's own poetry, then we can gain a higher insight into the verse structure. The universal or the general is always paramount in our reading of the poet's works. Book titles like *The Labyrinth*[34] or *The Narrow Place* carry with them the sense that something on earth is what is being talked about, as well as a sense that perhaps the metaphor has been used with other areas of existence in mind. Often the narrative line in Muir is obscured by our consideration of symbolic implications, as in "The Human Fold:"[35]

> Here penned within the human fold
> No longer now we shake the bars,
> Although the ever-moving stars
> Night after night in order rolled
> Rebuke this stationary farce.

32. Ibid., p. 123.

33. Ibid., p. 124.

34. *The Labyrinth* (London: Faber, 1949).

35. "The Human Fold," pp. 99–101.

One has a sense here of some of the problems posed by Kafka with respect to the cosmos or a divine order; but what is missing is the sense of being haunted, the hallucinatory overtones, that are always present in Kafka's work. Life is the same kind of reality for Muir as it was for Kafka—but Muir's feelings and thoughts carry us farther. What Muir might call the "sense of the road" comes out in some of the same ways in the "journey poems" of *Journeys and Places* and in his poems exploring directions and migrations of the self or of others. Many of these latter are in *The Voyage.*[36] The frustration of the hero in Kafka is usually in terms of what the protagonist wants, or what he does not know that he wants. These dramas are present in Muir—but in Muir it is the actual nature of the relationship of the poetic personal voice to the divine orders that is such a powerful theme. In Muir's use of general, metaphysical language, he seems at odds with his more imagistically orientated contemporaries. In speaking of Kafka's "serious fantasies," Muir was also being highly descriptive of his own metaphorical creations. Thus, Muir, like Kafka, had to make up his own "fable"—had to create or remake the language in order to understand what he had to understand in terms of life or poetry. It was necessary to express his own unique way of looking at the physical universe. To read Kafka or Muir without an active imagination—a tolerance—is a mistake.

"To Franz Kafka" suggests another facet of Muir's creative works in relation to Kafka. Possibly fascinated by Kafka's almost Calvinist obsession with fate in human life, Muir, in one of his better poems, praised Kafka's honesty and lack of sentimentality:

To Franz Kafka

If we, the proximate damned, presumptive blest,
Were called one day to some high consultation
With the authentic ones, the worst and best
Picked from all time, how mean would be our station.
Oh we could never bear the standing shame,
Equivocal ignominy of non-election;
We who will hardly answer to our name,
And on the road direct ignore direction.

But you, dear Franz, sad champion of the drab
And half, would watch the tell-tale shames drift in

36. *The Voyage and Other Poems* (London: Faber, 1946).

> (As if they were troves of treasure) not aloof,
> But with a famishing passion quick to grab
> Meaning, and read on all the leaves of sin
> Eternity's secret script, the saving proof.

Edwin Muir must also have felt regret at the fact that Kafka died so early. Perhaps writing the poem was a kind of act of personal apology to purge his own sorrow and his feelings with respect to the novelist's death. Kafka was indeed the "sad champion of the drab"; and in a tribute to Kafka's humanity Muir states that Franz Kafka was quick to

> read on all the leaves of sin
> Eternity's secret script, the saving proof.

In "Sappho"[37] the ancient Greek poetess was depicted as somehow being positively involved with the name-giving process. In the "place poems" reality was seen as being permeated with problems in spite of this. And in his translations of Kafka, Muir was seen to be attracted to a man who both dramatized the particular and added the nightmare element to his novelistic depiction of reality. As if to weave together all these strands, Muir wrote "The Transfiguration,"[38] a profound, serious examination of the problems of virtue and reality. In fact, one can speak of the poem, on its most important level, as adding virtue to reality, similarly to the way that some accounts of the resurrection of Christ add worth to human history. Central to Muir's considerations when writing the poem must have been the realization that such metaphorical construction might be useful to an age which is too prone to think in tragic terms. And furthermore, Muir must have been conscious of current ideas (as in the novels and essays of D. H. Lawrence) that a kind of self-effacing, masochistic, and self-imposed sexual puritanism had grown up in modern civilization.

Central to my consideration of the poem "The Transfiguration" is the idea of "positive metaphor"—the unabsolute idea that there are metaphors that are highly serious in nature, antitragic in tone, and "metaphysically romantic" in the poem. When we have identified and discussed the positive metaphors we will somehow be closer to the center of the real nature of "The Transfiguration." An awareness of these metaphors will suggest the broad-reaching implications of this work:

37. "Sappho," p. 131.

38. "The Transfiguration," pp. 198–200.

The Transfiguration

So from the ground we felt that virtue branch
Through all our veins till we were whole, our wrists
As fresh and pure as water from a well,
Our hands made new to handle holy things,
The source of all our seeing rinsed and cleansed
Till earth and light and water entering there
Gave back to us the clear unfallen world.
We would have thrown our clothes away for lightness,
But that even they, though sour and travel stained,
Seemed, like our flesh, made of immortal substance,
And the soiled flax and wool lay light upon us
Like friendly wonders, flower and flock entwined
As in a morning field. Was it a vision?
Or did we see that day the unseeable
One glory of the everlasting world
Perpetually at work, though never seen
Since Eden locked the gate that's everywhere
And nowhere? Was the change in us alone,
And the enormous earth still left forlorn,
An exile or a prisoner? Yet the world
We saw that day made this unreal, for all
Was in its place. The painted animals
Assembled there in gentle congregations,
Or sought apart their leafy oratories,
Or walked in peace, the wild and tame together,
As if, also for them, the day had come.
The shepherds' hovels shone, for underneath
The soot we saw the stone clean at the heart
As on the starting-day. The refuse heaps
Were grained with that fine dust that made the world;
For he had said, To the pure all things are pure.'
And when we went into the town, he with us,
The lurkers under doorways, murderers,
With rags tied round their feet for silence, came
Out of themselves to us and were with us,
And those who hide within the labyrinth
Of their own loneliness and greatness came,
And those entangled in their own devices,
The silent and the garrulous liars, all
Stepped out of their own dungeons and were free.
Reality or vision, this we have seen.
If it had lasted but another moment

It might have held for ever! But the world
Rolled back into its place, and we are here,
And all that radiant kingdom lies forlorn,
As if it had never stirred; no human voice
Is heard among its meadows, but it speaks
To itself alone, alone it flowers and shines
50   And blossoms for itself while time runs on.

But he will come again, it's said, though not
Unwanted and unsummoned; for all things,
Beasts of the field, and woods, and rocks, and seas,
And all mankind from end to end of the earth
Will call him with one voice. In our own time,
Some say, or at a time when time is ripe.
Then he will come, Christ the uncrucified,
Christ the discrucified, his death undone,
His agony unmade, his cross dismantled—
60   Glad to be so—and the tormented wood
Will cure its hurt and grow into a tree
In a green springing corner of young Eden,
And Judas damned take his long journey backward
From darkness into light and be a child
Beside his mother's knee, and the betrayal
Be quite undone and never more be done.

The poem, as the title implies, is a deeply felt, religious work of art. In point of fact the language is so sensuous, so elemental, that with some alterations and the omission of several phrases, it could easily be regarded as another great love piece—a poem celebrating an event in the cycle of a love experience, that is, sensuous ecstasy, and the complete transformation of the self with a consequent deep merging with the world. I would suggest that Muir's ability to transform the Biblical transfiguration into the significant event that he does may stem from memory of a love event in the poet's past life that he was or was not conscious of as he wrote this religious work. Perhaps his ability to write the verse as he does derives from the quality and memory of such an experience. The tone is that of the great middle love poems.

The title "The Transfiguration" is very important if we are to assign properly what is denoted by the "we" of the first line. By the fifth word of the poem we become aware that we are listening to either one of the disciples, or a kind of Greek chorus of disciples describing the nature of an event, or anyone directly involved with a savior's life, or finally a voice that is in some way representative of all men. In case the significance of the event has eluded us if we have not been paying enough attention, Muir pulls us into the scene of action. A miracle, by its very nature, confounds our notions of reality or possibility and takes us away from our ordinary way of looking at things. It is renewing in itself, but even more it has a tendency to draw us away from ordinary reality, from ourselves. In this way Muir immediately lets us escape ourselves and creates a condition of wonder in which the poet's imagination leads us on. But always at the back of this poem (and even at the end of it) are the terror and the pressure of our real lives—in contrast to the miracle of escape, the miracle of change. The tones of bitterness and regret are very important, but not dominant, thematic threads.

A tree begins from the ground and has branches—and the human body is almost thought to be a tree, at the beginning of the poem. This metaphor is reinforced by the elemental words "ground," "branch," "veins," and "wrists." The body itself has been transfigured by Christ into something pure and complete in itself. Something has begun, again, from the ground up—a kind of inner resurrection based upon the whole physical body. The resurrection of the self stretches outward. The natural function of seeing lets in the ancient elements themselves. This is not a blank slate, but the wholeness of the sensuous self; the transfiguration is sensual and spiritual and extends beyond the self. The freshness and purity remind one of the whiteness of Christ's figure in the Bible. (It is perhaps appropriate to mention that only one adjective of color appears in the poem, despite its deep sensuality.) "Christ" was prefigured in the title, and already we have a vague identification with those components of the poem that have to do with "nature," "man," and "self." Like the inside of many modern Catholic churches in France, the imagery of the first sentence is sparse, clean, and vigorous, the logic flawless. This concrete spareness is reflected in the conservative use of the iambic line. The first seven lines have served as a kind of musical statement, sufficient and unique in itself, and prefiguring the rest of the poem.

The next sentence of the poem takes us beyond the mere abstraction of the miracle itself. Lines 8 through 13 add a sense of rebellion to the verse and freshen our modern understanding of the Biblical miracle—an underlying purpose of the entire poem. People think about throwing away their clothes when they are in love and in sensual touch with each other, or when there has been a profound spiritual awakening. The former phenomenon (sensual attraction) combined with the latter (movement of the "soul") is, of course, one of man's greatest emotions. And for Muir the transfiguration is seen to have this miraculous effect upon the beholders.

Along with the heightening of the theme of transfiguration, it might be said that the verses from "We would have thrown our clothes away" to "Was it a vision?" free us of our sense of sin in regard to sex. The reference to clothing should remind us of Eden, and the transfiguration here is seen to have accomplished the miracle of sensual purification. Through the eye, we have been cleansed of corruption and stupidity by a kind of inner action which can be similar only to the restorative action of sex. And yet it is better than sexual experience because we are not left with the harsh adjustments that must be made after the glow wears off. The event itself has made our clothing and flesh seem like immortal substance.

> And the soiled flax and wool lay light upon us
> Like friendly wonders, flower and flock entwined
> As in a morning field.

Muir asks us if this was a vision—this divine revelation. In a sense the poet answers us without being contemptuous of the question. The experience of the transfiguration is brought into relation with the cosmos itself in lines 14 through 18. The question is significant in its doubt and relates eventually to the "Some say" of line 55, serving as a kind of introduction to the second section of the poem. This passage provides a good example of a form growing out of an interrogative.

Also, man emerges from the muck of psychological interpretation as the poem develops in the section from "Or did we see" to "And nowhere?" Man's potential is seen as infinite, perhaps, as the result of the divine gift; yet we are still locked in this prison, with the world still around us—for Muir and the disciples a world within a world. But for the disciples the ordinary world is transfigured—a startling notion. Our curiosity is aroused by their vision, and the parts of the poem immediately following this question are concerned with working out the consequence of this one glory. Also, the sense here of seeing something not seen since Eden is magnificent in its evocation of vast distance and time. The phrase "the gate that's everywhere/And nowhere?" carries us considerably beyond the realm of the scripture writer into that of the poet. The simplicity of the next question is astounding and takes us beyond the mere relation of ourselves with the disciples. We shout in their faces. The earth was alone, a prisoner; yet at the same time—again a hint—these men, because of the shared perception of the Christ's divine nature, are able to partake of the divinity, which seems to linger in vague ways and stop at no specified time—a lack of explanation which is not consistent with the strict logic of the poem and is, it seems to me, a weakness. But perhaps this is not an important criticism. So Man has truly escaped from himself, and the temporary escape hints at another entire order of experience.

The world (lines 20 through 22) was still caught in time, but it did not seem this way to the disciples; Muir tantalizes us as he plans and imagines what the disciples saw. In lines 22 through 40, the poem switches from the relatively abstract to the concrete. First there is the metaphor of sequential place in the journey from the hill, through the country, by the huts on the road, to the outskirts of the city, and then to man himself in the city—as he is in the city. Note throughout this section the concreteness and vividness of the imagery: Muir was a vital man, and this particular variation on the story of Christ is vital in the best, most adequate sense of the word. In the course of the journey from country to town we move successively through animate, inanimate, and human nature. Note that nowhere in the poem is there a single note of regret; Muir did not regret life.

The painted animals are representative of inanimate nature. The synthesis and balance here of opposites remind us of at least one facet of Walt Whitman's thought. I like the movement in lines 22 through 26: from the group to the individual, and then to a reconciliation with life. Note that it seemed for the painted animals, also, that the "day had come"—knowing and not knowing. Man is above and yet below, and this takes us beyond mere escape from ourselves—a theological concept, no doubt, that I have been too long ignorant of. Note that images of inanimate nature begin to be *gently* diminished here, and that roles of man become ascendant. We encompass yet transcend the stinking refuse heaps. We find quite simply "we went into the town" (after lingering, again gently.)

Here we find man. This entire passage is reminiscent of the form found in section 5 of Yeats's "Nineteen Hundred and Nineteen" and also of the *Inferno*. The murderers—those of us who destroy willfully (all of us)—along with the lurkers "came/Out of themselves." At poles, yet similar in inner state, the lonely and the great *only* come. A line stops at "all," and it relates back to the stop at "came." And then the housewives and liars and the silent—still all of us—"Stepped out of their dungeons." "Reality or vision," (it does not matter, the terms have become synonymous) "this have we seen."

Next come two passages that are reminiscent of T. S. Eliot's "The Waste Land" except that there is less agony, less bitterness (Muir saves these for later). I am not really sure of the tone of lines 43 through 49. One notes that the silence is deafening—in passing. I believe that we hear the voice of the disciples after the experiences with Christ. Note that they are gentle, kind, slightly reflective, and innocent. Time has passed. But twenty centuries have passed since we lost our chance. This is the conception that Muir is ready to give to us. And it is for this reason that the gigantic pause has occurred. We are to ruminate, take stock; note, in passing, the quiet pause after "stirred."

Muir is developing the idea of what would happen if Christ should return in an uncrucified condition. Instead of being a social disturber, the Christ who will return will be welcomed by nature, animals, and men. Our condition will resemble that of man as he was in Eden; even the greatest sinner of all time, Judas, will be redeemed from time.

At the level of myth, or at the level of operation on our consciousness, the poem moves in several ways. In the first seven lines the appeal is to the idea of wholeness, health, and well-being essential to the good life. Lines 8 through 13 appeal to our perennial hope that we (all mankind) can abolish the terrible things in us or the effects of terrible events of the past that have shrunk and deformed us; the poem suggests the possibility of doing this. The myth of Christ is essential for the understanding of the next several lines, which develop the possibility of this transfiguration of all men occurring for a short time through Christ before his betrayal—or through stories of the resurrection of Jesus after the crucifixion. A pleasing archetypal sequence in this same section, as compared with the opening of the poem, is a movement from personal concern to a concern for men at large ("when we went into the town" and what follows). In lines 43 through 49 we are back in what is man's ordinary condition here; the power of this short section appeals to the archetypes of the ideal and the actual. Finally, in the second and last stanza of the poem, the appeal is to the fundamental idea of a future better than the present, extended in the poem to the idea of personal or even historical redemption for all men, past and present. The poet also makes use of material from other myths, such as that of Eden in line 17, adding his own vision to improve upon and discuss the significance of the Biblical account of Jesus of Nazareth. Thus, Muir can create new metaphorical combinations that appeal to fundamental archetypal emotions in the human sensibility, as well as add elements of wonder and fascination to the old stories. He can use past myths, as well as his own understanding of his own experience, to create poetry that, in its depth, itself serves the function of religion and mythology.

VII

Last Poems

Those poems of Edwin Muir that were collected after *One Foot in Eden*[1] and published in the Oxford University Press edition of 1965[2] are less centered upon concepts and ideas such as "place," "journey," "time," or "history." Some of these last works rather take up religious ideas; others consider social and political phenomena; yet others deal with psychological ideas. They can also be said to be characterized by concern with the individual's relation to reality. One has a continual sense of the artist approaching death, with a concomitant questioning capacity developing as time passes. We find this questioning, doubtful quality in the opening stanza of "Sonnet" ("You will not leave us"):[3]

> You will not leave us, for You cannot, Lord.
> We are the inventors of disloyalty,
> And every day proclaim we dare not be
> Ourselves' or Yours: at every point absurd.
> For this was forged the counterfeiting word
> By which the hours beguile eternity
> Or cry that You are dead Who cannot die.
> So in a word You are glorified and abjured.

It is not inconceivable that saviors such as Jesus might regret their time on earth. Man, through his capacity for memory, keeps the saviors in mind. Thus one aspect of a savior (our impressions of him) is with most of us, so that such a savior is, in a sense, not entirely free, not entirely eternal. Even with this strong bond, man, in the second through fourth line, is not

1. *One Foot in Eden* (London: Faber, 1956).

2. *Collected Poems* (New York: Oxford University Press, 1965).

3. "Sonnet" ("You will not leave us"), p. 257.

capable of the achievement required by great religions. "Absurd" can
be seen as carrying existential weight, in that the word was current in
European intellectual history when Muir used it. Probably the poet meant
the particular sense of the absurd dichotomy between what is and what
ought to be, or the breach between the actual and the ideal. The poet then
moves on in the next four lines to a consideration of "God's death" (as is
implied in the work of Friedrich Nietzsche). Christ was crucified as if in
answer to the glory he might have brought about. Such are the ways of
men. Yet this very fact clears Christ of responsibility for the existence of
evil, for he does not appear as all-powerful. He died through his ultimate
failure to control human action. In short, he was like humanity in every
sense of the word. Through our consciousness of Christ's idealism and his
practical capacities he is "glorified." Through his humanity—his inability to
cope with the problem of evil by eradicating it (as symbolized, unfortunately, by his death)—he becomes human and therefore partially "ab-
jured" of responsibility.

"The Song,"[4] which follows "Sonnet" is the first indication that Muir
might be grappling with the problem of saviorism as metaphor. In these
poems Muir is saying. "Well, if we want a savior, let's look at what he
might be like in modern poetry, which, for the most part, through its
interest in logic, language, and meaning, goes deeper than modern theological concern: let's see what he would be like." One can only regret not
having what might have come into being if Muir had lived to see these
poems in final form, had lived to write the whole book (all the poems), and
had lived to name the work. One can speak of Pound's *Cantos* as providing
an artist's view of human life and history; one can speak of Muir's last
poems as providing a pattern for history itself. The poet is moving very
deeply, and on very sensitive ground, throughout this final section of
poems.

In "The Song" Muir delves into the worlds of dream and vision:

> I was haunted all that day by memories knocking
> At a disused, deaf, dead door of my mind
> Sealed up for forty years by myself and time.
> They could not get to me nor I to them.
> And yet they knocked. And since I could not answer,
> Since time was past for that sole assignation,
> I was oppressed by the unspoken thought
> That they and I were not contemporary,

---

4. "The Song," pp. 257–259.

> For I had gone away. Yet still in dreams
> Where all is changed, time, place, identity,
> Where fables turn to beasts and beasts to fables,
> And anything can be in a natural wonder,
> These meetings are renewed, dead dialogues
> Utter their antique speech.

In *An Autobiography* Muir had discussed a condition wherein he had had conscious visions:

> The analysis was very painful, then, especially for the first few months; so much stuff gushed up from my dreams that the effort of facing it was a prolonged nervous and moral strain. I fell into a curious state, and had trances and visions. My unconscious mind, having unloaded itself, seemed to have become transparent, so that myths and legends entered it without resistance and passed into my dreams and daydreams. This happened a few weeks after the beginning of the analysis, and it began with a feeling that I had caught some illness; this in turn passed into a trance.[5]

In the case of "The Song," however, the past has entered into consciousness during the day before sleeping: at night the poet "dreams." Memory, acting also, probably, in conjunction with immediate problems, produced the dream vision of the beast in the park at night: "Where all is changed, time, place, identity." Earlier experiences described in *An Autobiography* run along similar lines with the story of "some great beast":

> The day I remember best was the day when Freddie Sinclair chased me home: it was after we had gone to Helye, and his road lay in the same direction as mine. He was the boy I had fought over the knife, and this day he wanted to fight me again, but I was afraid. The road from the school to Helye lay on the crown of the island, and as I ran on, hollow with fear, there seemed to be nothing on either side of me but the sky. What I was so afraid of I did not know; it was not Freddie, but something else; yet I could no more have turned and faced him than I could have stopped the sun revolving. As I ran I was conscious only of a few huge things, monstrously simplified and enlarged: Wyre, which I felt under my feet, the other islands lying round,

5. *An Autobiography* (London: Methuen, 1968), p. 159.

the sun in the sky, and the sky itself, which was quite empty. For almost thirty years afterwards I was so ashamed of that moment of panic that I did not dare to speak of it to anyone, and drove it out of my mind. I was seven at the time, and in the middle of my guilty fears. On that summer afternoon they took the shape of Freddie Sinclair, and turned him into a terrifying figure of vengeance. I felt that all the people of Wyre, as they worked in their fields, had stopped and were watching me, and this tempered my fear with some human shame. I hoped that none of my family had noticed me, but when they came in from the fields at tea-time Sutherland said, "Weel, boy I see thu can run!" I had got over my panic by then, and pretended that Freddie and I had been merely having a race. Sutherland laughed. "Ay, a fine race, man, a fine race!" He called me 'man' when he wanted to be sarcastic.[6]

The dream, in the case of "The Song," by being a dream, has the effect of renewing the elements of the poet's guilt with respect to being careless. Muir might not have walked in the field with the bull to begin with; he might not have associated with Freddie Sinclair. The prose passages present warnings and lessons with respect to the unpredictability of "human beasts." The nature of bad friendships or friendships temporarily gone sour is also a key area of exploration. Muir might have reflected in later life that a more adequate human being might have taken proper action to avoid the trances and the bad early experiences described in these prose passages; he may have decided on a poem where the same lessons could be taught without a description of an unpleasant, earlier series of events. One learns through experiences. In later life one goes more out of one's way to avoid the unpleasant if at all possible (one tries to do this without becoming sentimental). In the realm of psychological or dream terrors, unpleasantness or evil is perhaps more difficult to avoid, for in that world one still seems to find elements of lack of control even if one's waking life is pleasant. By depicting the dream or psychological sphere of action, Muir extends the realm of poetry into that of dreams. There is little doubt about Muir's intent. The poet says openly "That night I dreamed." The beast can be symbolic of those bad things in life that should be avoided; yet such things, even if passed by or avoided, linger in the sense that we are conscious of them, or else the bad things can invade our dream life. The poet seems to

6. Ibid., pp. 42–43.

suggest that through proper "diplomacy" we can avoid much that is evil. By using the matter of dreams and its undeniable psychological realism, the author lends credence to stories of monsters or the Biblical beast:

> Was it these hoofs, I thought, that knocked all day
> With no articulate message, but this vision
> That had no tongue to speak its mystery?
> What wound in the world's side and we unknowing
> Lay open and bleeding now? What present anguish
> Drew that long dirge from the earth-haunting marvel?
> And why that earthly visit, unearthly pain?
> I was not dreaming now, but thinking the dream.
> Then all was quiet, the park was its own again,
> And I on my road to my familiar lodgings
> A world away; and all its poor own again.
> Yet I woke up saying, 'The song—the song'.

The last line of this poem may be seen in two senses: the human being has a natural tendency or instinct for affirmation: secondly, the "song" (something meaningful and beautiful) is far away and not present at all—the call for a "song" is based on mere memory, or hearsay. A third meaning is possible: the "song" in itself (perhaps the dream) is awful. The poem, insofar as it discusses the nature of a possible savior, can be seen as comparative, for it is involved in a realm dealing with a figure who would be concerned with saving *all* mankind from itself.

The religious poems "The Church"[7] and "Salem, Massachusetts"[8] are clear, straightforward, and concrete, probably stemming out of the Muirs' experiences in America:

Salem, Massachusetts

> They walked black Bible streets and piously tilled
> The burning fields of the new Apocalypse.
> With texts and guns they drove the Indians out,
> Ruled young and old with still Hebraic rod,
> The Puritan English country gentlemen;
> And burned young witches.

7. "The Church," pp. 262–264.

8. "Salem, Massachusetts," p. 264.

                          Their sons' grandsons
Throve on Leviathan and the China trade
And built and lived in beautiful wooden houses,
Their Jordan past.
                          You may see the Witches' Trail
Still winding through the streets to a little knoll
That looks across a tideless inland bay
In the clear New England weather. This they saw,
The women, till the fire and smoke consumed
Sight, breath and body while the Elders watched
That all was well and truly consumed by fire.
The House with the Seven Gables is gone, consumed by fire,
And in the evenings businessmen from Boston
Sit in the beautiful houses, mobbed by cars.

The sequence in lines 3 through 6 carries from "Indians" to "young witches" as objects of attack. One might think of the "Indians" not only as victims of conquest of the West, but also as people who in their finer moments were in close contact with nature. The "young" and the "old" might be thought of as those more likely to be rebellious or gay—as well as most likely to be subject to middle-aged peers in society. The "stiff Hebraic rod" seems anti–Song of Songs, and anti–Greek; The "witches" might be the equivalent of modern lady beatniks, lay hippies, or female rebels. As for "The Church":

                This autumn day the new cross is set up
                On the unfinished church, above the trees,
                Bright as a new penny, tipping the tip
                Of the elongated spire in the sunny breeze,
                And is at ease;
                Newcomer suddenly, calmly looking down
                On this American university town.

We are reminded in the next stanza that the cross, "this archaic trick,"

                Brings to the heart and the fingers what was done
                One spring day in Judaea to Three in One;

Perhaps more significant in stanza 3 is the fact that

> Nature cried
> To see Heaven doff its glory to atone
> For man, lest he should die in time, alone.

The "crib, the desert, and the tree" call up successively birth and child-hood, the period of intensive labor (for many) in young and early man-hood, and finally the period in the late twenties and onward when one can enjoy the fruits of one's labors more fully. Muir speaks of "the Church, that stretched magnificence" as magnificent insofar as it provides symbolic representation of the finer, greater, more valuable aspects of life. The phrase "splendour of blue and gold" calls up the elements of tragedy and conflict (as well as a more positive manifestation) inevitable in the assumption of humanity by an omnipotent diety. This phrase has involved a changing around and summing up of Byzantine history: One does think of the blue and green factions in Byzantium. With the "blue and gold" we think of this, and also the fact that in the West blue can be associated with Mary, and therefore birth, and gold often with the inlaying cross of Pre-Renaissance and Renaissance painting. By speaking of "that splendour of blue and gold" instead of "blue and green" the poet seems somehow to lessen our consciousness of Christ's suffering, and also, in the same way, the suffering that goes along with our sensitivity to the factionalism in the Eastern Empire. The blue suggests stability, endurability: the gold suggests worth and value. The last three stanzas of this poem are among Muir's best:

> What reason for that splendour of blue and gold
> For One so great and poor He was past all need?
> What but impetuous love that could not hold
> Its storm of spending and must scatter its seed
> In blue and gold and deed,
> And write its busy Books on Books of Days
> To attempt and never touch the sum of praise.
>
> I look at the church again, and yet again,
> And think of those who house together in Hell,
> Cooped by ingenious theological men
> Expert to track the sour and musty smell
> Of sins they know too well;
> Until grown proud, they crib in rusty bars
> The Love that moves the sun and the other stars.
>
> Yet fortune to the new church, and may its door
> Never be shut, or yawn in empty state

To daunt the poor in spirit, the always poor.
Catholic, Orthodox, Protestant, may it wait
Here for its true estate.
All's still to do; roof, window and wall are bare.
I look, and do not doubt that He is there.

The last two lines contain a great deal in a short space. Progress and
mythmaking are modern prerogatives for the church. The evidence speaking for the existence of God is perhaps nothing more than an act of faith in
the presence of so many intangibles in modern life; yet Muir, in this poem,
does not "doubt that He is there."

"An Island Tale"[9] and "The Two Sisters"[10] are about human love. Perhaps
of most significance is the way that the two poems develop the story of the
fate of feminine beings. They are highly moving in that they deal strikingly
with the way life treats women:

An Island Tale

She had endured so long a grief
That from her breast we saw it grow,
Branch, leaf and flower with such a grace
We wondered at the summer place
Which set that harvest there. But oh
The softly, softly yellowing leaf.

She was enclosed in quietness,
Where for lost love her tears were shed.
They stopped, and she was quite alone.
Being so poor, she was our own,
Her lack of all our precious bread.
She had no skill to offer less.

She turned into an island song
And died. They sing her ballad yet,
But all the simple verses tell
Is, Love and grief became her well.
Too well; for how can we forget
Her happy face when she was young?

9. "An Island Tale," pp. 266–267.

10. "The Two Sisters," pp. 281–282.

Perhaps part of the appeal of this poem stems from the contrast between what is usually the real situation, and what the situation is that is depicted in the poem. In life, loyalty in lost love to the point of complete withdrawal is rare; there are often short-term loyalties in love affairs, but the loyalty tends to diminish, in the ordinary case, and the individual affected tends to be drawn toward further possibilities for life. We learn for sure in the second stanza that the "grief" that had been seen to "grow" was due to a lost love:

> She was enclosed in quietness,
> Where for lost love her tears were shed.

The attitude of the female lover drew sympathy from people, perhaps because of its simple plainness of emotion ("Being so poor, she was our own"). The tragedy evoked a spirit of commemoration in art ("She turned into an island song"). The phrase "And died" summons up the idea of a purpose in life even for the tragic and betrayed insofar as they relate to other people's lives. But the poet is careful to remind us that

> all the simple verses tell
> Is, Love and grief became her well.
> Too well; for how can we forget
> Her happy face when she was young?

"The Two Sisters" is similar to "An Island Tale" in tone, and similarly makes use of death to end a summing up of a feminine life (or lives, in the case of "The Two Sisters"):

> Her beauty was so rare,
> It wore her body down
> With leading through the air
> That marvel not her own.

The first line is not unlike what one might expect from W. B. Yeats (a line in praise of a beautiful woman). The "beauty" is so delicate that she (in her possible forgetfulness and aesthetic sensitivity) is even more subject to what time, accident, and life may have in store for her. Then in the third line Muir manages to convey the sense of feminine beauty in motion. The poet conveys the sense of chance, willful breeding, or a deity, or a fated beauty with his talking about "That marvel not her own." The woman must have thought in terms of preserving her gift of beauty. She faced the

"enmity of change" and "time's incontinence/To drink from beauty's bone."
The other sister is not as fair ("That fault of hers") as the first one, but, as is
often the case in life, the implication is that she may have been more
happy, and perhaps through more required effort, more skillful in practical
matters. But even in the case of the second sister, "Grief and mismanage-
ment" "make an end of grace." She, like the first sister, is dead, or willing
to be:

> These ladies put to sea
> To join the intrepid dead.

As one looks at life, society, the world, and oneself, in the contemporary
nuclear world, one might be tempted to say at times, in frustration at the
nature of existence, "I'm tired of it. Why not blow it all up? Death couldn't
be any worse than this." As if in answer to this usually unspoken death
wish, Muir wrote "After a Hypothetical War."[11] In this poem there is "No
rule nor ruler," "only water and clay," and a "purblind peasant" who is
"never loved" and petty in his greediness. As for the landscape:

> There you will see
> The soil on its perpetual death-bed; miles
> Of mendicant flowers prospering on its bier,
> And weeds as old as time, their roots entangled,
> Murderer choking murderer in the dark,
> Though here they rule and flourish. Heaven and earth
> Give only of their worst, breeding what's bad.
> Even the dust-cart meteors on their rounds
> Stop here to void their refuse, leaving this
> Chaotic breed of misbegotten things,
> Embryos of what could never wish to be.
> Soil and air breed crookedly here, and men
> Are dumb and twisted as the envious scrub
> That spreads in silent malice on the fields.
> Lost lands infected by an enmity
> Deeper than lust or greed, that works by stealth
> Yet in the sun is helpless as the blindworm,
> Making bad worse. The mud has sucked half in
> People and cattle until they eat and breathe
> Nothing but mud.

11. "After a Hypothetical War," p. 265.

The poem, although highly naturalistic, can be read as if Muir were self-consciously writing in a spirit of complete contempt; the intended heavy and dark tone of Muir's lines is not dissimilar to that of Section III ("The Fire Sermon") of T. S. Eliot's *The Waste Land*. The poet goes on to point out that the human "cradle" is "an image of the grave." Ironically, and much too late to benefit the squatters and leftover people who asked the same question, the poet asks (as people presently ask about themselves), "What rule or governance can save them now?" We realize through this moral poem that, indeed, things would be much worse "After a Hypothetical War." In spite of the ugliness of the setting, the poem even may be optimistic with respect to the fate of the human race.

"The Last War"[12] is a more developed treatment of the theme of nuclear or ultimate warfare. The first stanza emphasizes the relatively helpless status of individual men in such a hypothetical conflict. It would appear as if there would be little in the realm of personal action that would affect possible outcomes once a nuclear war started:

> No place at all for bravery in that war
> Nor mark where one might make a stand,
> Nor uses for eye or hand
> To discover and reach the enemy
> Hidden in boundless air.

The *Iliad* presented a world where bravery, at times, could be seen as a virtue: the *Song of Roland* is called up by the "mark where one might make a stand"; "eye or hand" calls up still more primitive types of war, but in combination with the next two lines produces a consciousness of air warfare—a more modern phenomenon in many forms. The stanza closes rather pessimistically with the thought that "we are still in time for a little time." In the second stanza Muir asks if action is even worth while at all in such conditions as the present. If we diminish the stature of man there will be less ego battle; but perhaps we should not do this but think of our victories over other animals:

> Or shall we picture bird and tree
> Silently falling, and think of all the words
> By which we forged earth, night and day
> And ruled with such strange ease our work and play?

12. "The Last War," pp. 282–285.

In the third stanza the poet goes on to consider what might be the nature
of such a mass death:

> Perhaps nothing at all will be but pain,
> A choking and floundering, or gigantic stupor
> Of a world-wide deserted hospital ward.

After a comparison of man with refugees, Muir asks:

> Will great visions come,
> And life lie clear at last as it says, Good-bye,
> Good-bye, I have borne with you a little while?
> Or shall we remember shameful things concealed,
> Mean coldnesses and wounds too eagerly given?

The next two stanzas go on to ask important questions about our disaffec-
tion with the world, to seek a solution to the disharmony, and finally to
present a vision of the human life cycle:

> I thought, our help is in all that is full-grown
> In nature, and all that is with hands well-made,
> Carved in verse or stone
> Or a harvest yield. There is the harmony
> By which we know our own and the world's health,
> The simply good, great counterpoise
> To blind nonentity,
> Ever renewed and squandered wealth.
> Yet not enough. Because we could not wait
> To untwist the twisted smile and make it straight
> Or render restitution to the tree.
> We who were wrapped so warm in foolish joys
> Did not have time to call on pity
> For all that is sick, and heal and remake our city.

V

> About the well of life where we are made
> Spirits of earth and heaven together lie.
> They do not turn their bright heads at our coming,
> So deep their dream of pure commingled being,

So still the air and the level beam that flows
Along the ground, shed by the flowers and waters:
All above and beneath them a deep darkness.
Their bodies lie in shadow or buried in earth,
Their heads shine in the light of the underworld.
Loaded with fear and crowned with every hope
The born stream past them to the longed for place.

In Yeats's "The Tower," there is the "stronghold never taken," the
stronghold being the nature of one's self; the poem considers a human life
defying all efforts of men. Yeats's "Tower" stands in opposition to the
forces of destruction from within or without. By contrast, Muir's "The
Tower"[13] is clearly delineated as a Tower of Babel in the opening sentence.
"The Tower" seems problematical in a new way—but in point of fact there
is nothing new under the sun. The structure is built by men:

Oh, that the clouds would bear it away.
When our morning stint is done
We watch the mannikin sentries stand
Shoulder to shoulder with the sun
(They are like tribesmen of the air)
And view the geometrical line
Of shadow cutting in two our land.
What have we fashioned but a sign?

A wealth of thought is summed up on the last line: *homo loquax* overcomes
homo sapiens. The poet passes on to images of brute nature to emphasize
man's inhumanity, or his tendency to destruction: the "empty sign" seems
indicative of a spiritual or intellectual hollowness. The "clouds" assume an
importance in the last five lines of stanza 1 as the poet asks "What are our
masters? Who are you there?" The Biblical legend of a single language common to men before their dispersal is reflected in the second section:

This is the old men's story. Once
Voices were there, resounding words
Of an incomprehensible tongue
Fit for great heroes and great lords,
But never spoken anywhere.
And once a simple country song
Began and suddenly ended.

13. "The Tower," pp. 278–279.

Muir is quite bitter about only "a dead lord" who "flutters down" as recompense for the lost Eden. He asks in closing about a world of immortality (a different world) and asserts our existence with a finality that could be viewed as tragic:

> *So* look the dead
> Whose breath stopped on a different star.
> Who are they? We are what we are.

"The Poet" is one of Muir's most concise, clear, and revealing works— it deals primarily, and rather introspectively, with what is involved with a poet himself when writing poetry. The principal subject matter is the writer himself:

The Poet

And in bewilderment
My tongue shall tell
What mind had never meant
Nor memory stored.
In such bewilderment
Love's parable
Into the world was sent
To stammer its word.

What I shall never know
I must make known.
Where traveller never went
Is my domain.
Dear Disembodiment
Through which is shown
The shapes that come and go
And turn again.

Heaven-sent perplexity—
If thought should thieve
One word of the mystery
All would be wrong.
Most faithful fantasy
That can believe

> Its immortality
> And make a song.[14]

It is with a sense of mystery and "bewilderment" that the poet begins to create. One should note that Muir rather hopefully uses the future tense in the first stanza; "tell" strikes us with the sense of "relating a tale." What is being told is in the realm of "What mind had never meant"; in other words, the poet in the creative act must transcend the mind's own powers. There is a kind of Faustian tone about these lines. In the fourth line memory is seen as capable of being disconnected from what is summoned up by the poet. The process—indeed, even the product—has even with the most precise, accurate interpretation a sense of the unknown; yet the product is seen as "Love's parable." In spite of the mystery of the world, the mysteries of poetic processes themselves, poetry can be seen as the Word. The poet therefore, paradoxically, makes known what he "shall never know"; in spite of the sense of mystery a form of knowledge is obtained. Instead of being blind like ancient Homer, the modern poet has a sense of metaphysical and intellectual "bewilderment." The true poet is seen as an explorer in territory where no one has gone before. By always being a journeyer, the poet is somehow disembodied from home territory, or perhaps even the essential things of life—the central experiences. The poet is in an area where "shapes...come and go/And turn again." For the poet poetry and life are a "Heaven-sent perplexity." Even if one could steal a glimpse of ultimate truth, it would appear, as if bewitched, "wrong." Indeed, in a world and universe where nothing is certain our poetic couplings with life are "faithful fantasy." The poetic world—that is, the final written product—is a kind of dream. Yet there are elements of truth about it. Also, the poet, because he has this "faithful fantasy," can believe in his own immortalilty as a poet, or a more metaphysical kind which might make life worth while. Thus, the poet goes on to manufacture a song, and by so doing joins the many thinkers who have written about the creative process. By calling the poem "The Poet," Muir isolates and examines one part of himself: the poetic self, which, as manifested in a body of poetry, may often be very different from the everyday self, the real psychological self, or the self of one's realm of action.

"Dialogue" ("I never saw...") is an unusual poem in theme. A possible interpretation might go like this: Making use of the poet's voice, the poet in the first stanza speaks of someone else—a male—in praise of that

---

14. "The Poet," p. 286.

person's effect on him. In contrast to this is the voice of a girl or woman, who had a much different experience with the same person. The earlier tone of approbation is such that the poet sounds as if he might be addressing a figure such as Christ, Buddha, or Mohammed. The experience is not dissimilar to that of "The Transfiguration." The later comment of the woman becomes most dramatic:

Dialogue

I never saw the world until that day,
The real fabulous world newly reborn,
And celebrated and crowned on every side
With sun and sky and lands of fruit and corn,
The·dull ox and the high horse glorified,
Red images on the red clay,
And such a race of women and men,
I thought the famous ones had never died.
I speak in truth of what he showed me then.
But you whom he loved and yet could never dare
To win, how was it that you did not care
For such a man as he?

　　　　　"Oh he was dull,
Sick of the cheats of his phantasmal art
And that unending journey through no place,
He said, and asked to fly into the cool
And subterranean harbour of my heart,
Darker than his, more cool. He little thought
It was a riotous prison that he sought,
A place indeed, but such a place!
What could he give me, who was never his fool,
Nor Helen, nor Iseult, playing a harlot's part?
I have wondered what he read into my face."

I knew a man, the most unlike that one,
I think the shrewdest, sweetest man
I ever saw, modest and yet a king
Among his harvests, with a harvester's eye
That had forgotten to wonder why
At this or that, knowing his natural span,
And spoke of evil as "the other thing,"
Judging a virtue as he judged the weather,
Endured, accepted all, the equal brother

Of men and chance, the good and the bad day.
And when I spoke of the high horse glorified,
He smiled and answered: Tell me, will it pull?
Or find its way in the dark? Is it on my side?
Then I'm its friend. But it must answer
To bit and rein. I do not want a dancer.
And yet he loved a good horse as a good
Workman or field or block of seasoned wood.
He was neither a plain nor a fanciful fool.
Yet that first world was beautiful
And true, stands still where first it stood.

"I have known men and horses many a day.
Men come and go, the wise and the fanciful.
I ride my horse and make it go my way."[15]

The "bewilderment" in the poem "The Poet" has vanished, and what we
have on the part of the poet is a new ability to see things as they are: "The
real fabulous world newly reborn." Life is now seen to be a kind of celebration, an activity of divine right. One's relation with the fundamental raw
material of life, such as "sun" and "sky", is seen to be altered (we are
reminded of Mallarmé's *azur).* We move with the experience of transfiguration through uncultivated and cultivated inanimate nature, from the
common, hard-working beast of burden, (the ox) to "the high horse" whose
relevance to men is more aesthetic. Women and men are so fabulous that it
appears as if "the famous ones had never died." These transfigurations are
seen to be the result of someone showing the poet how to relate to reality.
Exactly who this person is is never specified; it does seem to be someone
extraordinary—a saint, a savior, or an excellent friend. With the last three
lines of the first stanza the author introduces us to the female who "did not
care/For such a man as he." The woman sees the same figure the poet has
praised as "dull,"

> Sick of the cheats of his phantasmal art
> And that unending journey through no place,

As the woman saw it, her own role was nothing more than serving as an
escape for this person. That woman, rather attractively and modestly,
demonstrates the nature of her own soul as something to escape to:

15. "Dialogue," pp. 287–288.

> What could he give me, who was never his fool,
> Nor Helen, nor Iseult, playing a harlot's part?

Then, somewhat puzzled, she asks: "I have wondered what he read into my face."

The following stanza is couched in terms that one usually reserves for the most profound of friends. For the poetic voice of Muir the "man" was shrewd and sweet—that of a successfully active man, and a man who looked death in the face. He "spoke of evil as 'the other thing,'" and judged virtue for what it was. He

> endured, accepted all, the equal brother
> Of men and chance, the good and the bad day.

In completing his eulogy, the speaker asserts

> he loved a good horse as a good
> Workman or field or block of seasoned wood.
> He was neither a plain nor a fanciful fool.
> Yet that first world was beautiful
> And true, stands still where first it stood.

There is an element of refreshing detachment in the girl's or woman's final words:

> I have known men and horses many a day.
> Men come and go, the wise and the fanciful.
> I ride my horse and make it go my way.

This dialogue, about love, and personal differences with respect to impressions, with its implications about how a man and woman can react differently in more general ways, is very serious if we keep in mind the idea of a "savior figure" that may run through all these poems. If we also keep in mind the myth of Judas, we can take the poem as a warning with respect to trying to do the right thing at all times in a very, very tricky century in which to be alive. In more simple terms, and perhaps more accurately, the poem can be seen as a serious psychological examination of both the speakers as well as of their subject.

A poem that raises equally serious and painful questions is the "Ballad of Everyman." It seems to be a poem that should be read by everyone

throughout the world, and although it may be unfinished, it is one of the
greater modern poems. Such a poem might help to heal the wounds of our
modern world (assuming, perhaps incorrectly, that idealism has any place in
international relations).

Ballad of Everyman

I

Stout Everyman set out to meet
   His brothers gathered from every land,
And make a peace for all the earth
   And link the nations hand to hand.

He came into a splended hall
   And there he saw a motionless dove
Swung from the roof, but for the rest
   Found little sign of peace or love.

Two days he listened patiently,
   But on the third got up and swore:
"Nothing but slaves and masters here:
   Your dove's a liar and a whore.

"Disguised police on the high seats,
   In every corner pimps and spies.
Goodbye to you; I'd rather be
   With friends in Hell or Paradise."

The great room turned to watch him go,
   But oh the deadly silence then.
From that day brave Everyman
   Was never seen by friend again.

II

Night after night I dream a dream
   That I am flying through the air
On some contraption old and lame
   As Icarus' unlucky chair.

And first I see the empty fields—
   No sign of Everyman anywhere—
And then I see a playing field
   And two great sides in combat there.

And then they change into a beast
  With iron hoofs and scourging tail
That treads a bloody harvest down
  In readiness for the murdering flail.

And then a rash of staring eyes
  Covers the beast, back, sides and head,
And stare as if remembering
  Something that long ago was said.

And the beast is gone, and nothing's there
  But murderers standing in a ring,
And at the centre Everyman,
  I never saw so poor a thing.

Curses upon the traitorous men
  Who brought our good friend Everyman down,
And murder peace to bring their peace,
  And flatter and rob the ignorant clown.[16]

It is probably no accident that a poem so idealistic, and yet in parts so profane, was found in unpublished manuscript. Muir, having lived a long time, was aware of the way that life often deals with ideals such as those expressed at the end of stanza 1. By using the figure of Everyman from the English tradition, Muir speaks of everyone, yet of a single person at the same time. Most modern people have politically oriented thoughts of how the "potential hell in the air" might be dealt with, as well as the terrible sporadic outbreaks of violence, or even the virtually full-scale war around us (if such may be the case). This poem serves to remind us that in a serious activity such as trying to save the world there are both inner and outer obstacles—problems of personal limitation, as well as the problems and nature of the Other. Most people discover this early.

Muir, as it were, acts out with his figure of Everyman some of the cross-purposes and themes involved in saving the world, whether it be an individual or a group that is being talked about. I know of no other modern poem with such essential, potentially dangerous, potentially beneficial content. One is indeed in the same sort of realm as was the writer of the stories of the Biblical antichrist or risen Christ. Everyman, now coupled with the dilemma of our age—our possible destruction—cuts quite a figure in the first stanza. We have a portrait of an idealist—a political idealist (not unlike Hölderlin in "Hölderlin's Journey"). Such quixotism appeals to Muir,

16. "Ballad of Everyman," pp. 290–291.

yet at the beginning of section II he rather disclaims responsibility by describing himself as viewing the scene

> On some contraption old and lame
> As Icarus' unlucky chair.   .

If one can think of two Christs—Christ the tiger, and Christ the meek—one is not too far off in what is being gotten at in this second section of the poem. But by talking about "two great sides," the poet involves us all. The "great sides" change into a beast, which is in turn metamorphosed. The poet, like the maker of films or the abstract painter, can manufacture his own reality or realities:

> murderers standing in a ring,
> And at the centre Everyman.
> I never saw so poor a thing.

Everyman is at last caught in the corruption that he had so bravely condemned.

> Curses upon the traitorous men
> Who brought our good friend Everyman down,
> And murder peace to bring their peace,
> And flatter and rob the ignorant clown.

In "Nightmare of Peace"[17] Muir again makes use of the Everyman/beast theme. The central idea in this poem is that when Everyman comes he offers something to the world; but at rebuffs he indeed becomes a beast. "Nightmare of Peace" is particularly effective insofar as it sums up an atmosphere that was present in the world of the late fifties and early sixties:

> Even in a dream how were we there
> Among the commissars of peace
> And that meek humming in the air
> From the assenting devotees?
> Police disguised on every chair
> Up on the platform. Peace was there
> In hands where it would never stir.
> Aloft a battle-plated dove
> Throned over all in menacing love.

---

17. "Nightmare of Peace," pp. 291–293.

Everyman appears, but leaves, and the poem goes on to answer the question posed by the first four lines. The poem is a kind of depiction of a "world nightmare"—a nightmare that can be seen to stem out of the anxieties of living in a nuclear age:

> Then it came:
> A slowly lengthening horrible tail
> Thrust from the ambiguous monster's back,
> The calmly lazily waving thing
> That brushes flies on a summer day.
> A beast trampling as oxen tread
> The annual yield, the harvest play.
> For a moment: then we saw the lies
> Spring open, watched the rows of eyes
> Break out upon the animal's back.

"'I Have Been Taught'" is placed, appropriately, at the end of the Oxford *Collected Poems* of 1965, and the phrase "time grows shorter" at the first line of the fifth stanza indicates that Edwin Muir was conscious of growing old, and perhaps even his imminent death. The poem serves, probably intentionally, to sum up a lifetime:

> "I Have Been Taught"
>
> I have been taught by dreams and fantasies
> Learned from the friendly and the darker phantoms
> And got great knowledge and courtesy from the dead
> Kinsmen and kinswomen, ancestors and friends
> But from two mainly
> Who gave me birth.
>
> Have learned and drunk from that unspending good
> These founts whose learned windings keep
> My feet from straying
> To the deadly path
>
> That leads into the sultry labyrinth
> Where all is bright and the flare
> Consumes and shrivels
> The moist fruit.
>
> Have drawn at last from time which takes away
> And taking leaves all things in their right place

> An image of forever
> One and whole.
>
> And now that time grows shorter, I perceive
> That Plato's is the truest poetry,
> And that these shadows
> Are cast by the true.[18]

In an age highly influenced by the psychoanalytic doctrines of Freud and Jung, Muir acknowledges his debt to what one learns about oneself and others through examinations of one's dreams and waking dreams. He also acknowledges his debt to those already dead—probably through the examples of their lives as well as through what has been left behind. The poet has learned from relatives, dead relatives, friends, and, most importantly, his parents. In the second stanza he speaks of goodness as if it really exists in both an absolute sense and in the forms of its particular manifestations:

> That unspending good
> These founts whose learned windings keep
> My feet from straying
> To the deadly path

Muir acknowledges a kind of divine justice in the form of

> time which takes away
> And taking leaves all things in their right place
> An image of forever
> One and whole.

In this stanza, Muir goes beyond mere glimpses of immortality or shadows of a true "image of forever"; his is a vision of enduring reality. The poet comes to recognize that

> Plato's is the truest poetry,
> And that these shadows
> Are cast by the true.

18. "I Have Been Taught," p. 302.

VIII

Conclusions

Time, one of Muir's favorite themes, is treating Edwin Muir as well as he himself treated it in his poetry, and the general consciousness of this humble, mild-mannered, and honest man's voice is gradually increasing. In Muir we are finding a different kind of voice—a quieter and more puzzled voice than is to be found among his great predecessors.

I think a sense of reasoning that there are gaps in our ability to speak poetically for our own time has a lot to do with Muir—a man whose consideration by scholars and critics seems somehow to be bound up in the attempt to find a different pageant. Critics would agree that perhaps more than 80 per cent of Muir's best poetry was published after he was fifty years old—a fact that Muir, his wife, and J. C. Hall have subscribed to also in that about 250 out of approximately 300 pages of the Oxford edition of the 1965 *Collected Poems*[1] appear to contain poems written in Muir's late forties until his death in 1959 in Cambridge at the age of seventy-two. Thus at the side of Thomas, and then later in the late fifties with Graves and Ian Hamilton Finlay, Muir was one of the more important producing figures, a fact which was generally recognized first among younger English poets in the early sixties whom he had considerable influence over, a group of scholars, and then rather tardily, and perhaps reluctantly, by an Eliot who had ceased to sound like his old self in poetry ever since the *Quartets*, but who had enough wisdom to preface Muir's 1965 *Collected Poems*. In fact, one can think of only a few English poets whose older age was as productive.

In certain ages there have been different sets of accepted theological standards or general laws, grouped according to regions, countries, or continents. With the existence of such universals—that is, the acceptance of a myth or set of symbols to explain man's behavior or place in the

1. *Collected Poems* (New York: Oxford University Press, 1965).

universe—poetry for the writer or believer can be an exploration of these generally accepted truths, or points where the poet mildly or intensely feels that the prevailing mythological framework is missing. The inner assurance may create both a stability and, at the same time, a concern that is not very exploratory in nature. There might even be a general sanction against exploration—such as the concept of heresy. The troubadours present examples of several groups of poets who felt fairly sure about the larger questions and therefore were induced to confine themselves to an exploration of a singular secular theme such as love. Or, like Dante, they could explore the moral and personal significance of the prevailing mythology. Both the forces shaping the poet and the way he reacts to them can be felt consciously or unconsciously.

Such a stable climate for poetry seems to me to be in sharp contrast with what the conditions for modern poets have been in this century. Unsure of his knowledge of the universe, and lacking sanctions from sources that could be generally accepted, the poet has often had to explain the universe for himself. Often myths accepted in youth have had to be discarded as the poet's perception of the present has become too complex. What had been adequate became inadequate. Lacking believable universals, the poet still felt an acute need for them; so he searched, sometimes unconsciously, for these truths in his poetry. Muir, for one, had been reasonably sure when he was younger. Losing faith as a result of subsequent events, he still felt the need of a kind of synthesis similar, in terms of assurance, to that of his youth. Most of us grow up in urbanized areas without even a sense of the need for stability. But someone like Muir was lucky enough to enact the general historical movement of the last two centuries from certainty to insecurity in the span of his early life. This would eventually be reflected in the poetry, and explains much of his universal significance. Muir was indeed fortunate to have grown up in Orkney, a region where there was a generally accepted body of local myth in the form of ballads and fabulous stories:

> The Orkney I was born into was a place where there was no great distinction between the ordinary and the fabulous; the lives of living men turned into legend.[2]

This tradition may not have been as completely developed as the Christian one was in the Middle Ages, but it was adequate enough for his youth, and also strong enough so that throughout his life, after leaving Orkney, Muir was conscious enough of his past to have a sense of what was now

2. *An Autobiography* (London: Methuen, 1068), p. 14.

missing from his life. In later life he was always searching for the integration and exploration that he had experienced in his youth. A contention—
indeed, the primary contention of this critical work—has been that
consciously, or unconsciously, Muir was searching for a mythological
integration with his environment. The absence of a universal mythological
sanction enabled Muir, along with other modern poets, to enter unique
areas and employ unique perspectives. This quest resulted in a poetry that
everywhere seems to demonstrate the presence of profound moral and
aesthetic seriousness before the facts of life. This is not to say that all of
Muir's poetry is necessarily myth; but often it is. The very fact that many
serious people in the modern world have turned to poetry rather than to
theology can hardly be insignificant in regard to this last point.

Thus, perhaps more than any other recent modern poet, Muir came to
feel keenly—although not wholly to share—the mythological or theological
uncertainty of his age. Not only does the poet reflect man's unsureness in
the face of the universe, but a later, more mature resolution with respect to
a course of action occurs in *One Foot in Eden*[3] and in the last poems, in
that Muir seems particularly and singularly more preoccupied than earlier
with creating metaphorical structures that can be used to create an ordered
relationship between the self within and the world without. What Muir
has written in the entire body of his works is not merely a poetry that
can be called more mythological than others, but also a specific type of
poetry that may be called "mythological poetry" in that it is more concerned than the poetry of the past in terms of language and content with
what might be called pure metaphysics in philosophy—specifically the
concerns with the nature of time, space, creation, eternity, history, man's
destiny, personal psychology, and the structure of the universe.

Such poetic structures serving as a guide to the outer world seem closely
related to ideas of the same general historical era as that of Schopenhauer
about art objects being escapes from the world of will in the sense that
they reflect or are very close to the world of ideas, the Platonic forms
beyond forms, or the will world's essential constitution. Art was seen as
being close to the ultimate nature of reality. Also, Muir seems to transcend
the aesthetic ideas of Hegel about a kind of absolute art, in that the poet
comes back to tackle reality, and not ignore it as Mallarmé tried to in
Un coup de dés. I mean by this that history or reality is approached and
undergoes a fundamental transmutation through the poet's skill with the art
object.

It seems as if the world that embroidered the love poems of the Eliza-

3. *One Foot in Eden* (London: Faber, 1965).

bethans has suddenly become the poem itself, and the poet uses his art to create a structure that mediates between his own soul and the world. When a universal genius forms this meditation in the very language of philosophy and myth, pregnant with human thematic material, the result might be called "mythological poetry" or "absolute emblems." Muir might indeed be talking about his own poetry when he speaks of the value of an emblem as a device to be used for accurate historical knowledge and its uses:

> You will be with space and order magistral,
> And that contracted world so vast will grow
> That this will seem a little tangled field.
> For you will be in very truth with all
> In their due place and honour, row on row.
> For this I read the emblem on the shield.[4]

Perhaps it would be appropriate to draw a brief distinction among meditative, epic, and mythological poetry. Meditative, religious, or mystical poetry is perhaps closest to the type of poetry I am trying to define. But what I think of as meditative poetry usually involves a personal relation to a deity whose reality is accepted or debated, and this god's existence is a prior assumption of the poems. "God" is seen as an omnipresent being threading itself throughout the context of the verse. The poetry is thus connected with the idea of a god, and it is usually the product of a man whose civilization, region, or cultural institution accepts a conception of a god or gods. The poet's relation to God is the source of the drama. The poetry of St. John of the Cross is a good example. The successful epic poem usually has at least three dominant characteristics: it is long, it is narrative, and it often expresses the dominant features of an era or civilization. Also, it seems to assume that man can act out a destiny here on earth. This is the poetry of Homer, Virgil, and Milton. In "mythological poetry," sureness about the existence of God is subordinate to questions or concerns that are more directly related to comcepts of history, psychology, time, space, and dreams, as well as to man's personal relation to these things. What distinguishes this poetry from the epic is that it tends to be shorter, as well as being the product of a civilization to which man more is a foremost concern. It is probably shorter because unity has given away to a relative complexity, so that man can see more ways to reproduce more experiences, rather than a general and single way. Man and his individual cosmological experience are more important than a god or a whole civili-

4. "The Emblem," pp. 230–231.

zation. This is the poetry of Rilke in the *Duino Elegies*, the secular epics of Robinson Jeffers, the emblematic poetry of the later Edwin Muir. At least some poets would say that philosophers like Kant, Hume, Schopenhauer, Nietzsche, and Marx, as well as the onslaughts of scientific thought, have rattled the old gods and created a metaphysical and philosophical junk pile. Such poets are forced to write a poetry of metaphysical exploration in order to define a place for man in the universe. All poetry can indeed be used by the reader as myth—and has been; but the idea of a poetry that is more mythical in form and content than others has been realized in the last hundred years.

In discussing a book by David Daiches, *The Novel and the Modern World*,[5] Muir sees a certain incompleteness inherent in Daiches's view that the chaos of contemporary civilization ("we are living in the midst of the disintegration of a civilization"[6]) has resulted in a unique literature. He also objects to another of Daiches's claims that for the literary work

> What the real work is and what gives the principle of organi-
> zation to the whole can be certainly determined only by investi-
> gating the relation of the printed words to the civilization that
> produced them.[7]

It is clear to Muir that these views may result in an overemphasis of historicism. So he counters the views of Daiches with this:

> The writers of this century have certainly been troubled by
> the problem of an era of transition; but it is clear that they have
> also been troubled by the desire to convey a new sense of
> experience.[8]

Here, Muir stresses individual talent.

I would suggest that Muir himself has been very successful in conveying just such a sense of new experience to the modern reader. And it is this new experience, coming with a consciousness of the older experience, that makes Muir so important. In contrast with many of his contemporaries, Muir did not have a formal education. Instead, he created his own means

5. Daiches, David, *The Novel and the Modern World*: (Chicago: University of Chicago Press, 1939).

6. Ibid., p. 223.

7. Ibid., p. 217.

8. *Essays on Literature and Society* (Boston: Harvard University Press, 1965), p. 141.

of educating himself. The result, in his case, seems to be a much healthier, sounder, and more natural relation to tradition than many of his fellow poets were able to achieve.

As I suggested in the opening remarks of this book, Muir's capacity to see the world in a very wide manner, and from the viewpoint of a fundamentally virtuous man, was unique among his contemporaries. His experiences in translating Franz Kafka meant that he dealt most closely with a writer who may come to be regarded as the most expressive of modern man's sense of nausea at the nature of the world. Muir can be seen as filling in many of the holes that Kafka was conscious of or created. Muir was therefore able to press forward into areas that are usually the province of myth. The absence of certainty meant that the poet could be a legislator of reality. Yet, at the same time, Muir's thorough grounding in tradition enabled him to transcend his early unhappiness—the angry young man of *We Moderns*.[9] By forging new myths about the modern world, concretely constructed on the basis of the older universal realities, he became both a poet and mythmaker.

By challenging the nihilist's view of man Muir was able to move closer to a truer picture of man as he exists in the modern world. In one of Muir's best essays, "The Natural Man and the Political Man,"[10] he sees the natural man of Lawrence, Hemingway, and Montherlant as well as the political man of fascism or communism as being both somehow less in stature than the man of tradition; the latter is a combination of rationality and emotion, spirit and body, as distinct from these lesser modern types who are merely mechanical bodies or socially processed robots. At the close of the essay Muir sees Wordsworth as unique among the modern writers as perhaps the last major example of a man who had the true balance of the classical stance. Muir says of Wordsworth's poetry:

> For it records a moment of mystical co-operation between reason and impulse, man and nature; it does not describe a process, or make a general statement about life which can be embodied in a theory. It is rather the outline of a possibility, and the record of moments in which that possibility was realised. But Wordsworth's followers vulgarised his conception of nature, and reduced to a dogma what to him had been an illumination; and between them with their crude faith in mountains and

---

9. *We Moderns* (New York: Knopf, 1920).

10. *Essays on Literature and Society*, pp. 150–164.

woods and the evolutionists with their benevolent universe evolving towards even greater benevolence, there was an intellectual and emotional affinity. Both of them, unintentionally, helped to set the moving principle of good outside man, and in doing so helped to dehumanise experience and history; whereas Wordsworth was essentially concerned with the mind of man and its capacity to respond to the mighty sum of things for ever speaking. In the response lay the cooperation between impulse and reason, and the possibility of harmony; without the response there was no harmony, and it could not be created by means of a theory concerning it. But the theory, nevertheless, dominated the nineteenth century, and has extended its influence over ours.[11]

Muir could indeed be speaking about his own virtues and his own difficulties with things. Not only is he a figure with stature in English literature; he is also, as I hope can be seen in these pages, a figure worthy of examination in the context of world literature. This latter evaluation is particularly true if we keep in mind the nature of Edwin Muir's themes.

Indeed, his own comment of Joyce's *Finnegans Wake* and Ezra Pound's *Cantos* is worth repeating:

It is clear that the two works just mentioned are not deliberately obscure. They express things of the greatest importance to their authors, and express them with extraordinary if sometimes perverse skill. This being the case, why should we not understand them perfectly? It may be partly because Joyce and Pound are so concerned exactly to express what is in their own minds that they forget the reader; so that the more precise, the more impenetrable they become. But one feels more is involved than this. There seems to be a rule by which, in our time, the more an imaginative work of art contains, the less it communicates. The more the writer tries to render his vision of the world in its completeness, the more irrevocably it turns into a private world. The more carefully he connects everything with everything, the less able his reader is to connect anything with anything. Joyce's world seems to be complete, but the reader is not in it and cannot get into it. He sees it as a child might see a globe of the world before he is able to read, pleased by the colours of the

11. Ibid., p. 164

different countries and the shapes of the continents, but convinced that it is all a private secret known only to his elders.[12]

Muir's poetry can be thought of as more "available" to the general reader than most—and this fact perhaps made this comment inevitable.

Poetry is as much a matter of choice of theme and craft as of thought. Muir's relation to the best literature of the West is very significant, and I hope that by suggesting the nature of some of the content of the poetry as well as its relationship to Kafka, I have also indicated some of the points of contact between Edwin Muir and the literature of the past. If one thinks of the 1965 *Collected Poems* as an autonomous whole in itself one has a correct way of starting to think about Muir. As I have indicated, Muir may be seen as analogous to Franz Kafka in many of his attitudes—and insofar as Muir wrote poetry in which positive values were directly emphasized and celebrated, he often transcended Kafka. But perhaps of equal and final significance is Muir's comment upon Kafka as a craftsman:

> Temper, method, style; all are consummate. His diction is of the utmost flexibility and exactitude, and of an inevitable propriety. His conduct of the sentence is masterly. Flowing without being monotonous, his long sentences achieve an endless variety of inflection by two things alone: an exact skill in the disposition of the clauses, and of the words making them up. I can think of hardly any other writer who can secure so much force as Kafka by the placing of a word. Yet in all his works he probably never placed a word unnaturally or even conspiciously. He had, it seems to me, all the intellectual and imaginative as well as the technical endowment of a great writer.[13]

In spite of the fact that Muir is discussing Kafka, it may be helpful to conclude with the suggestion that we may take this paragraph as epitomizing his own ideal of poetic achievement.

12. "Correspondences," *Observer*, No 8422 (2 November 1952), p. 9.

13. "A Note on Franz Kafka," *Bookman*, (N. Y.) 72 (November 1930) p. 241.

Appendix I: Muir and the Critics

The nature and appeal of Muir's work have been the most important factor in the rise of his reputation; but the warm reception offered by discerning critics in the late fifties and the sixties has been a factor as well. The fact that Muir's poetry was published in his later years by Faber (a firm with which one associates T. S. Eliot) must have helped his cause considerably. The first *Collected Poems: 1921–1952*[1] appeared in 1952 in Great Britain with the Faber imprint, and the confidence of critics and readers must have been enhanced by Eliot's preface to the 1965 *Collected Poems*:

> And as I have grown older, I have come to realise how rare this quality is. That utter honesty with oneself and with the world is no more common among men of letters than among men of other occupations. I stress this unmistakeable integrity, because I came to recognise it in Edwin Muir's work as well as in the man himself.[2]

In further tribute:

> Edwin Muir will remain among the poets who have added glory to the English language.[3]

The publication in Great Britain in 1965 of the *Selected Poems*,[4] edited by T. S. Eliot, added further prestige to Muir's name. The paperback edition of

1. *Collected Poems: 1921–1952* (London: Faber, 1952).

2. T. S. Eliot in Muir's *Collected Poems* (New York: Oxford University Press, 1965), p. 3.

3. Ibid., p. 4.

4. *Selected Poems* (London: Faber, 1965).

the *Collected Poems*,[5] published in the early years of the quality-paperback boom, had helped Muir in America, and his appearance at Harvard in the 1955–1956 academic year, to deliver the Charles Eliot Norton Lectures, commanded further respect. In Britain, J. C. Hall's pioneering pamphlet in the Writers and Their Work series in 1956,[6] gave Muir an early push and enhanced the poet's reputation, as did full-scale articles in the United States by Fred Grice in 1955[7] and Charles Glicksburg in 1956.[8] His later reviews in *The Listener*[9] from 1932 to 1958, in *The Observer*[10] from 1924 to 1958, and in *The New Statesman*[11] from 1919 to 1959 kept him in the public eye in one sphere more than is the case with many poets. According to J. C. Hall, it was only after the publication of *The Labyrinth*[12] in 1952 that Muir was recognized as an important voice by more than a minority of critics in England.[13] The reappearance in 1954 of the respected and popular *The Story and the Fable*[14] (1940) in a new form, as *An Autobiography*,[15] must have helped a great deal to familiarize readers with the poet. And with the 1962 publication in the Evergreen Profile Series of P. H. Butter's well-written study,[16] analyzing Muir's work from the viewpoint of the New Criticism, Muir received the book-length consideration he deserved. In the

5. *Collected Poems* (New York: Grove, 1957).

6. J. C. Hall *Edwin Muir*, Writers and Their Work no. 71 (London: Longmans, 1956).

7. Fred Grice, "The Poetry of Edwin Muir," *Essays in Criticism* 5 (1955), pp. 243–252.

8. Charles Glicksburg, "Edwin Muir: Zarathustra in Scotch Dress," *Arizona Quarterly* 12 (1956), pp. 225–239.

9. Listed in Mellown, *Bibliography of the Writings of Edwin Muir*, pp. 79–115.

10. Ibid., pp. 69–116.

11. Ibid., pp. 59–116.

12. *The Labyrinth* (London: Faber, 1949).

13. Hall, *Edwin Muir*, p. 7.

14. *The Story and the Fable* (London: Harrap, 1940).

15. *An Autobiography* (London: Methuen, 1968).

16. Peter Butter, *Edwin Muir* (New York: Grove, 1962).

sixties, in full-scale articles by the poets Kathleen Raine,[17] Elizabeth Jennings,[18] and Thomas Merton,[19] three of the most important poets younger than Muir wrote about him in a single decade.

It is appropriate to speak of Thomas Merton, a poet associated with the monastic habit; before his death in 1968, he provided us with several acute insights into Muir's modes of thought and their manifestations in poetry. Merton's "The True Legendary Sound: The Poetry and Criticism of Edwin Muir" was published in the *Sewanee Review* in 1967. The monk established his continuity with what is becoming the principal thread in Muir scholarship: the fact that Muir looked at both intellectual and empirical reality in such a fresh and poetically compatible way that he cannot be ignored by anyone taking modern poetry, or life itself, seriously. As Merton sees it,

> Muir is one of those who intuitively realize that the giving of names is a primordial metaphysical act of the human intelligence— the Edenic office of the poet who follows Adam and reverifies the names given to creatures by his first father.[20]

Merton hints at a postexistential opening for a poet like Muir who looks at things so freshly and uniquely—the poet steps into some of the "philosophical gaps" created by the great doctrines of Sartre.

> The poetry of Edwin Muir gives evidence of profound metaphysical concern: concern for the roots of being, for being in act, manifested by numinous and symbolic qualities. He does not seek these roots out of curiosity, nor does he find them in speculative and dialectical discussion.[21]

He is, rather, one who reaches toward

17. Kathleen Raine, "Edwin Muir: An Appreciation," *Texas Quarterly* 4 (1961), pp. 233–245.

18. Elizabeth Jennings, "Edwin Muir as Poet and Allegorist," *London Magazine* 17 (1960), pp. 43–56.

19. Thomas Merton, "The True Legendary Sound: The Poetry and Criticism of Edwin Muir," *Sewanee Review*, 75 (1967), pp. 317–324.

20. Ibid., p. 317.

21. Ibid., p. 317–318.

the intimate, that is ontological, sources of life which cannot be clearly apprehended in themselves by any concept, but which, once intuited, can be made accessible to all in symbolic and imaginative celebration.[22]

And

Muir's metaphysical insight into the numinous and sacred which does not underlie but actually *is* the ordinary reality of our world, was not an other-worldy mysticism.[23]

Not only has the poet named some important things and provided glimpses of the sacred, but the very nature of what he has named is central.

As a poet he struggled to get the archetypes under control by means of the most obvious and familiar forms. He wanted to get the big symbols out and make them clear.[24]

Thus Merton sees the poet's imagination as acting to produce a sense of unity between what is outside one's self and what is within, and at the same time coming to terms with the present and the past.

In the poetic imagination the heroes of Homer and the Biblical patriarchs not only manifest themselves and make themselves comprehensible to the poet and reader, but they "coexist" with him.[25]

And a higher moral purpose is involved:

Muir is concerned with imagination not only in order that there may be good poetry, but in order that man himself may survive.[26]

Also, according to Merton, Muir's poetry expressed something that could not have been said any other way—and it is precisely this uniqueness that explains the relevance of the Scotsman.

Elizabeth Jennings is close to Thomas Merton in her Christian interpretation of Muir, and her intelligent examination of the poetry is partic-

22. Ibid., p. 318.

23. Ibid., p. 320.

24. Ibid., p. 321.

25. Ibid., p. 322.

26. Ibid., p. 323

ularly welcome since she has emerged as one of the leading female poets of her own generation. She is comparable to Merton in her concern and appreciation of Muir's metaphysics, but her tone is that of a Christian layman, as distinct from a monastic.

> Muir was a visionary poet whose poems were both the source and the fulfilment of his vision; they did not crystallize a past experience but embodied it even while it was being experienced. There was no question of feverishly seeking for appropriate imagery. The poetic, but also the visionary, experience came to him *in terms of* imagery. This is true of every poet but it needs to be remembered in any examination of the work of a visionary or mystical poet; for we tend to think that mystical poetry differs from other poetry in that the poet first experiences and afterwards searches for suitable imagery. This is not so at all. The vision *is* the words and images and only through them can it transcend them.[27]

We can see here that "imagism" (if there was ever such a thing) is extended to a definition of a type of "religious poetry"—the concretion of the mystical experience at the very moment of its occurrence in poetry. The last sentence is perhaps the most significant, when it is read along with the first sentence; although what we have here may be too narrow a definition of what might be called "visionary poetry," Jennings's description provides a successful and skillful working tool and is a real insight into the essential "isness" of the poems.

Jennings goes on to see Muir as close to the life of nature:

> The simple, primitive life of the soil, the immediacy of the changing seasons, the closeness of animal life, made a profound impression on him.[28]

One feels that she is struck by the quality of the abstraction (the "vision") in Muir's imagery, as well as by the concreteness; it is not merely nature's presence in the subject matter, but also the fact that the theme is involved with qualitative generalization as well as qualitative specificity, that is important. We can see that our "visionary poet," in his choice of subjects and in the outlining of the metaphysical wheels and the earth itself, is thereby touching the perennial universals—such as time—that nature offers. But more than this (more than just time),

27. Jennings, "Edwin Muir as Poet and Allegorist," p. 43.

28. Ibid.

Muir saw the life of mankind as an endless journey through
time, a journey continually repeating itself, continually reaching
again the same stages.[29]

Thus the poetry of Muir is seen as close to the recurring facts of each man's
or woman's life span in history—and in this journey through history in
time the ontological coldness and loneliness can be conquered:

Time is cold, pitiless—but it can be defeated; it can be defeated by being confronted with events outside time—by the
Incarnation, the Passion and the Crucifixion of Christ.[30]

One can escape from the hard logic of time (as Jennings sees it) through
the choice of Christian themes. By dealing with the language of Christ, by
providing the necessary data, by defeating time throughout the body of the
works, Muir thus "took the dogmas of Christianity and gave them a new
and dramatic life."[31]

Change, rebirth, decay, changelessness, place, original sin in connection
with the myth of Christ, childhood, the abuse of power, the duality of
flesh and spirit, love, and death all take their place in Muir's tapestry of
poetic language, according to Jennings. She almost says that our ability to
accept the archetypes may not necessarily work through the myth of
Christ, but rather may occur in a process where the individual becomes
conscious of the stillness and flux of poetic forms and archetypes—the
sacred language of poets like Muir. And to go beyond conceptions of
Christ and universals, she sees in the poetry a condition where

all is a movement yet all is also a stillness since repetition,
renewal and regeneration are signs of permanence.[32]

In connection with these ideas, Jennings sees Muir's contribution to the
English language as less spectacular, but perhaps as significant, as that of
Pound or Eliot—and she may feel that the nature of Muir's expression is
more important than any other.

Muir's achievement is to have examined and appropriated that
drama in intensely meditative but never merely abstract terms.

29. Ibid.

30. Ibid., p. 44.

31. Ibid.

32. Ibid., p. 45.

> The body of his work shows how a vision can often be most
> powerful when simplicity is at the centre of it—that simplicity
> which, as Eliot has said, costs 'not less than everything.'[33]

It is not really too far from here to regarding Muir as a mythmaker.

Kathleen Raine, in an attentive and inspired "Appreciation" of Edwin
Muir, seems less concerned with establishing the monastic or mystical
significance of Muir, as Merton did, or Muir's relation to the fundamentals
of lay Christianity, as Jennings was to do; rather, she saw Muir as being
more oriented toward expressing the harder-to-see side of a dual reality.
She sees the body of his poetry as being important because it expresses a
possible world behind the world we live in, a world of permanence as
distinct from a changing world, a world of immortality as distinct from one
of temporal existence. Her interpretation is not really very distant from that
of Thomas Merton or of Elizabeth Jennings. Discussing Muir's essay
"Against Being Convinced"[34] Raine takes up Muir's contention that philosophers cannot answer the question "What is life?"

> Though he [Muir] does not say so, he implies, I think, that
> to answer this question belongs to the poet; the poem communi-
> cates life, essence, which is indefinable; for the opposite of the
> philosopher, he says, would be "a thinker of an incredible
> simplicity, a spontaneity which would appear to be a piece of
> nature's carelessness."[35]

Speaking of the ways that poems either are faded by time or glow with
time, she sees Muir's poems in the latter category:

> Edwin Muir's poems belong, as it seems, to the second kind:
> time does not fade them, and it becomes clear that their excel-
> lence owes nothing to the accidental circumstances of the
> moment at which the poet wrote, or we read, his poems; they
> survive, as it were, a change of background, and we begin to see
> that whereas the "new" movements of this or that decade lose
> their significance when the scene changes and retain only a
> historical interest, Edwin Muir, a poet who never followed
> fashion, has in fact given more permanent expression to his

33. Ibid., p. 56.

34. *Latitudes* (London: Melrose, 1924), pp. 230–239.

35. Raine, "Edwin Muir: An Appreciation," p. 234.

world than other poets who deliberately set out to be the mouth-
pieces of their generation.[36]

The poet is seen as related to great modern mythological ideas such as
those contained in Jung's writings. According to Raine, Muir conceives the
"story" as the life of the individual, whereas the "fable" is the pattern built
up by the common, shared universal experience of the human race. It is
Muir's brilliant expression of the phenomena of this experience that explains his importance in connection with some of his younger contemporaries.

> Certainly Spender and Day Lewis felt strongly about world
> events; and Auden equals, indeed surpasses, Muir in descriptive
> vividness; but in Muir alone do we find "those hard symbolic·
> bones" that Yeats found in Dante and Blake—political poets
> also—that give form to events.[37]

Later, in the same vein, she sees Muir as discovering late

> what was known early to Dante and Milton, and discovered in
> the course of their poetic thought by Coleridge, Shelley, Blake,
> and Yeats, the great symbolic language of tradition."[38]

This juxtaposition of Muir with both modern poets and great poets of the
past is convincing and helpful, and Raine closes her article by showing that

> at his best, Muir achieved a poetic language at once powerfully
> mythological, yet concrete; symbolic, yet poignant with a
> particular joy or anguish.[39]

John Holloway, in a finely reasoned essay,[40] has insisted that Muir should
not be judged by superficial or fashionable standards. For Holloway, facile
reference to irony, concreteness, metaphorical life, vernacular strength, or
the "wit" of the thirties does not prepare the way for adequate recognition
of a poet of Muir's status and uniqueness; indeed, such concepts may be
terribly misleading.

36. Ibid., p. 233.

37. Ibid., p. 236.

38. Ibid., p. 243.

39. Ibid., p. 239.

40. John Holloway, "The Poetry of Edwin Muir," *Hudson Review* 13 (1960–1961),
pp. 550–567.

It is that in the end all these qualities are not the decisive signs of poetic achievement, but the subordinate and derivative ones. They are means to the major poet's ends, not the ends themselves.[41]

With this comment in mind, however, a reader of poetry might be led astray. Holloway says one might take "realism" too seriously, or, in contrast, one might go to the opposite extreme: to a sentimental, nonreferential excess of imagination. In both cases the result may be a fundamental hollowness and emptiness.

But the writer and the poet is concerned not only with the plain facts of what happens, of life; he is concerned also with the forces it holds in reserve, with its potentialities, its hidden strength for all that is remarkable, all that is good, all that is evil. This is why the poet—the poet particularly—may go in his work so far beyond anything that one could call a description of life in the realist's sense, that one begins almost to think that the interest of his poem can lie wholly in the intrinsic strangeness and newness of the imaginary world it describes; that its thrilling fantasy carries no reference back to our ordinary world at all. That is an error.[42]

Discussing the poems "Milton,"[43] "The Return,"[44] and "Telemachus Remembers"[45] in terms of the quality, importance, relevance, and centrality of their themes (death, the nature of a possible life after death, love, fidelity, and allegiance), Holloway comes to the conclusion that

the foundation of Muir's achievement as a poet is not a voguish manipulation of language, but the embodiment in verse of a deep and true apprehension of life.[46]

Thus Holloway establishes "a deep and true apprehension of life" as the

41. Ibid., p. 551.

42. Ibid., p. 552.

43. "Milton," p. 207.

44. "The Return," pp. 166–167.

45. "Telemachus Remembers," pp. 219–220.

46. Holloway, "The Poetry of Edwin Muir," p. 557.

principal criterion for judging the poems. It is the high seriousness of Muir's poetry that Holloway appears to admire particularly.

> We see craftsmanship as serving something greater than craftsmanship, serving in fact the new modes of vision of the poet which have led him to the new modes of being which he creates in his verse.[47]

Thus, central to Holloway's interpretation is the fact that the poet has created poetic landscapes of emotion and intellect that are the manifestation in verse of a serious and probing appreciation of human experience, as well as the fact that the poetry leads us to a fresh vision and therefore fresh experiences of reality.

Holloway goes on to assert Muir's high place among the political poets of the thirties—a role not heretofore emphasized. Poems like "The Labyrinth,"[48] "The Good Town,"[49] "The Combat,"[50] "Adam's Dream,"[51] "The Last War,"[52] and "Troy"[53] are seen to give Muir an elevated position, for in these poems it is not a matter of "models" (speaking of "Troy")

> of close sensuous observation or intricate concrete realization in a subtly interplaying verbal texture.[54]

It is rather the case that Muir, in the social poems, has

> broken through all this, as if through a surface: and has confronted us, by what is a kind of skeletal presentation, with the essential quality of a deeply disturbing reality.[55]

Going somewhat further than this, Holloway sees Muir as not being in

47. Ibid., p. 559.

48. "The Labyrinth," pp. 163–165.

49. "The Good Town," pp. 183–186.

50. "The Combat," pp. 179–180.

51. "Adam's Dream," pp. 210–212.

52. "The Last War," pp. 282–285.

53. "Troy," p. 71.

54. Holloway, "The Poetry of Edwin Muir," p. 562.

55. Ibid.

direct relationship with the French Impressionists and Symbolists. Instead, as a poet, he emerged from the horror, harshness, brutality, frankness and despair of German Expressionism—most significantly out of the labyrinthine nightmare world of Franz Kafka in *The Castle*[56] and *The Trial*,[57] which Muir translated (one might also mention Muir's translations of Lion Feuchtwanger, Shalom Asch, and Hermann Broch). According to Holloway, Muir observed, confronted, and reacted to the twentieth-century history and art of central Europe. As Arnold Toynbee might say, there were the real facts and those depicted—the preludes and the aftermaths: then there was an inevitable reaction, which is involved in Muir's poems. Or as Holloway puts it (in probably the best sentences ever written on Muir):

> The great central fact about Muir's work is that although in his vision of life the powers of evil were great, ultimately the powers of good and goodness were greater; and they were greater because they were also humbler, more primaeval, nearer to life in its archaic simplicity, which Muir was able to see not far below life's surface distractions. This, in the end, is the inner vision of joy which the iconic quality of his verse predominantly serves; and it is this sense of the simple but spacious powers of goodness held by life in reserve, that is ultimately what demands, and what justifies, Muir's simple but often monumental imagery; and his grave and lucid rhythms; and the honesty and spareness of his diction.[58]

Helen Gardner, seeing Muir as having evolved out of touch with the usual, ordinary educational experience (and thereby raising some questions about modern education), is struck by Muir's sweet temper and profound contact with the "nature of things and the destiny of mankind"[59] and by the high quality of his education of himself. We discover that he is one of the poets that she has "read and reread." For Gardner

> Muir's strength and distinction as a poet lie in his fidelity to his experience and in his conviction that that experience has a more than personal meaning. His poetry has an extreme purity of

56. Franz Kafka, *The Castle* (London: Secker, 1965).

57. Franz Kafka, *The Trial* (London: Secker, 1968).

58. Holloway, "The Poetry of Edwin Muir," pp. 565–566.

59. Helen Gardner, *Edwin Muir: The W. D. Thomas Memorial Lecture* (Cardiff: University of Wales, 1961), p. 11.

intention. It has no "palpable design on us." It states, or implies through images and symbols, convictions about the nature of things and the destiny of mankind. It is often content to state them simply, by rendering the image in its fullness. It gives us what he calls the "fable or myth of man" as glimpsed in the life-history of an individual of great intellectual integrity and rare spiritual sweetness and strength.[60]

To pick a particular example, Gardner sees an anology between Muir's sensitivity to animals as documented in *An Autobiography* (and poems like "The Combat" and "Horses"[61]) and Wordsworth's own reaction to mountains. But in Muir's case one has

> an extraordinary power of rendering, without the intrusion of adult feeling and adult reflection, the clear, bright, unmoral world of childish vision.[62]

She sees him as being concerned in the poetry with two great legends or myths in combination: the myth of the fall of man or expulsion from paradise, and the myth of universal purification. For Gardner, the early traumas in Muir's life through death in the family, general deprivation, and his own hard experiences from the time at the farm through his teens and twenties made him conscious of the story of the Fall of Man. Then a kind of reaction to a vision of original evil set in in later life:

> Both visions—of a fall from innocence to experience, an expulsion from Paradise, and of a redemption into a world that was not the world of childhood, but the world of man remade and glorified—were insistent visions.[63]

The visions were rather spontaneous, too, as Muir did move in the course of his life from the farm to the city, and then to some of the particular centers of European civilization. In the later years the immediate environment around him was more sedate and more civilized. In a way, he enacted the movement and development of civilization from the rural to the urban.

Gardner sees Muir as maintaining a lifelong poetic relation to the concept of eternal recurrence—the idea, in the most particular sense, that

60. Ibid., pp. 10–11.

61. "Horses," pp. 19–20.

62. Gardner, *Edwin Muir*, p. 14.

63. Ibid., p. 10.

life can be thought of as meaningless in that each "lifetime" involves the repetition of the same problems of life—and that one always recurs, always comes back to earth, back to time, and back to life without an escape from the process. Muir's poetry does not merely establish a context of meaning in relation to these ideas; it also deals with the problem unsentimentally. For instance, in "The Stationary Journey," imagination, although it possesses redeeming grace, is only

> A dream! the astronomic years
>   Patrolled by stars and planets bring
> Time led in chains from post to post
>   Of the all-conquering Zodiac ring.[64]

Central to Muir's deliberations on human process is a consideration of both play and serious action in man's life (as in place poems like "The Hill"),[65] as well as a consideration of manifestations of wisdom, knowledge of both good and evil, innocence, and "profound knowledge" in relation to the time process (as is carried out in poems such as "The Hill," "The Road" ("The great road stretched"),[66] or "The Mountains").[67] Gardner speaks then of Muir going beyond the mere naming, combining, and revivifying of some of our metaphysical categories and concerns. She sees him as dealing squarely with the realities of the dream process and then bringing these dreams to poetic life. In every case, this metaphysical and imaginative exploration is done with appropriate emotion and completeness:

> Wisdom, as distinct from knowledge, intellectual brilliance, or technical competence, is something we look for to poets, or should look for. He has great power to communicate, through the verbal recreation of visible and tangible experiences, invisible truths. Of all the poets of our century, none has, with less pretention or with more gentleness, made us more truly aware of the pathos, the grandeur and the mystery of our common humanity.[68]

---

64. "The Stationary Journey," pp. 57–59.

65. "The Hill," pp. 60–61.

66. "The Road" ("The great road stretched"), p. 223.

67. "The Mountains," pp. 59–60.

68. Gardner, *Edwin Muir*, p. 26.

Gardner's essay, in short, is primarily valuable for its knowlegeable general-
izations and the clusters of small insights it provides. It is metaphysical and
humanistic in its exploration of Muir's imagination, but its basic orientation
is not particularly religious.

R. P. Blackmur's essay "Edwin Muir: Between the Tiger's Paws,"[69] published in 1959, remains the most individualistic, as well as the most striking
and penetrating, critical work in the Muir canon. It is unique and highly
imaginative, containing a proliferation of insights into the poetry; it serves
as a reminder of how the best of the New Criticism helped the cause of
serious poetry in this century. Striking out at what he feels is the growing
professionalism of poetry, Blackmur sees in Muir simpler processes at work:

> The professional poet and his poetry should be seen as the
> collapsing chimaeras they mainly, and of necessity, are; then we
> could scratch where we itch. Then, too, we could enjoy for the
> hard and interesting things *they* are, the verses made by quite
> unprofessional poets like Edwin Muir out of honest and endless
> effort and the general materials of their language.[70]

To develop his growing vision of Muir, he suggests interesting comparisons
and contrasts between Virgil and the man from Orkney. Both men existed
at times of great empires, and in both men there was the existence of piety,
or *pietas*; Blackmur sees this latter quality as springing out of the resolution
of conflicts involved in the mutual cooperation that the existence of empire
itself involved. But Muir achieves a kind of "harmony" in his habit of
thought:

> This difficulty in achieving harmony indeed seems the
> characteristic difficulty of the human condition in our times, and
> it sometimes seems possible only to think it in verse.
>
> To say that this is what Muir has done, is another way of
> saying something about the attractive force of Muir's verse: he
> has made his harmony in the thought—not the numbers, the
> *thought*—of his verse: verse for him is the mode of his thought-
> ful piety, the mode of the mind's action where his piety is not
> only enacted for him but takes independent action on its own
> account and for us: when it does, it becomes poetry,[71]

69. R. P. Blackmur, "Edwin Muir: Between the Tiger's Paws," *Kenyon Review* 21 (1959),
pp. 419–436.

70. Ibid., p. 419.

71. Ibid., p. 421.

Deliberating on Muir's comments in *An Autobiography* about his life in Rome, Blackmur sees that the poet is particularly struck by the rage, terror, and human conflicts that have vanished while the still worthy products of that civilization (the architectural structures, for example) linger on. Blackmur speaks of the ruins and artifacts as a kind of allegory—suggesting that Muir's own verse is the modern equivalent of Roman ruins:

> The allegory which Rome provided for Muir out of the monuments and fountains of human· ruins and aspirations, and which he records in his prose, is a kind of prefiguration of the allegory—the effort to make things speak further for themselves than our mere words can signify alone—which he completes in his verse. I should like to point out that these allegories are not—as so many of our allegories are nowadays—puzzles or evasions or deliberate ambiguities or veilings of purpose, and they do nor require interpretation according to anything but the sense of intimacy in experience approached or observed with piety in order to accept what is there.[72]

Muir's language is the common educated language:

> I mean the allusions which are very nearly a part of the substance of our mind, so early were they bred in us by education and conversation: the allusions we can make without consciousness of their meanings, but which, when we do become conscious of their meanings, are like thunder and lightning and the letting go of breath.[73]

To illustrate the harmony and *pietas* as effects of Muir's poetry, Blackmur quotes from "The Good Man in Hell":

> One doubt of evil would bring down such a grace,
> Open such a gate, all Eden would enter in,
> Hell be a place like any other place,
> And love and hate and life and death begin.[74]

For Blackmur

> this looks backwards, through a little theology, into our most

72. Ibid., p. 423.

73. Ibid.

74. "The Good Man in Hell," p. 104.

backward selves where we abort, but need not, human action in
the hell of the wilfully wrong affirmation: it is that lethargy of
sensation, or boredom of perception, which feels only the wrong
good.[75]

In characters like Penelope, in "The Return," we find evidence of "great
tenderness" and "annunciation bringing incarnation." Such poems show us
the writer, Muir, as "like all of us in those moments when we put meaning
into our words."[76] The poems are, to Blackmur, "gestures of recognition"
and examples of "thinking in verse." They make

an old script, an older and different alphabet, out of the general
mystery and the common intuition, inescapably present, when
looked at, in our regular vocabulary of word and myth and
attitude.[77]

For further example, Blackmur reminds us that in "The Ballad of Hector
in Hades"[78] Muir attacks the racial nightmares through giving us their
therapeutic and reminding forms; in "The Enchanted Knight"[79] Muir
recognizes and indentifies a type of love in its perverse, narcissistic aspects;
and in a more general sense, a poem like "The Island"[80] extends justified
sympathy to a point:

> And simple spells make unafraid
> The haunted labyrinths of the heart,
> And with our wild succession braid
> The resurrection of the rose.

"The Annunciation ('Now in this iron reign')"[81] is seen to give an alternative
to dramatic evil in love. Everywhere in the poem is "pietas," a power of
generalization reminiscent of Emily Dickinson, and gesture that is morally
and aesthetically appropriate to the specific occasion. Muir emerges from

75. Blackmur, "Edwin Muir: Between the Tiger's Paws," p. 424.

76. Ibid., p. 426.

77. Ibid., p. 428.

78. "Ballad of Hector in Hades," pp. 24–26.

79. "The Enchanted Knight," p. 74.

80. "The Island," pp. 248–249.

81. "The Annunciation ('Now in this iron reign')," p. 117.

this essay as a poetic thinker on a par with Ezra Pound or T. S. Eliot, one who is engaged with the particulars of tradition in the most vital way. He has always an adequate vision, Blackmur points out, with respect to "pietas" and "harmony," qualities through which the moral, aesthetic, and religious foundations of his metaphor acquire an adequate stature.

A discussion in terms of the comprehensive and useful short critical study of Edwin Muir by P. H. Butter is most helpful at this point. Butter fills in facts about the poet's life, insofar as the life influenced the poetry. Born on a small farm in the Orkneys, the poet came to reflect in his poems "a sense of unity, of timelessness and of splendour."[82] These characteristics came from both the quality of the earlier family life, the natural identification of the child-poet with the country around him, and the freshness with which the child viewed reality.

> The journey out of Eden began at the age of six with the onset
> of a consciousness of change, of death, and of guilt.[83]

The family proved to be unable to cope with the problems of farming, and, by the onset of his teen years, Muir was living in Glasgow, an experience that hastened the progression from innocence to experience; the harshness of the urban environment and the conclusive breakup of the family heightened the stresses of the period for the young man. An interest in socialism and a respect for the ideas of Nietzsche—as well as an urge to self-education—characterized Muir in his twenties.[84] Shortly after meeting his wife and marrying, he moved to London and became an assistant on the *New Age*; by this means of employment he launched his career as a journalist. These events, his marriage, and his undergoing of complete psychoanalysis were the key happenings in his early thirties. After the summer of 1921 Muir and his wife were in Central Europe (Prague, Dresden, and Hellerau), and by 1924 they had started their translating activities. Most of the next 35 years were spent in England and Scotland, with prolonged periods in the south of France, Czechoslovakia, Rome, and America. According to Butter, Muir's full childhood, his experience of industrial life, his contact with culture in the great cities, his cosmopolitanism, the years of teaching, and his marriage combined to give him a good, full, and adequate life for a poet.

Butter goes on to deal with Muir's prose and poetry—assuming, perhaps

82. Butter, *Edwin Muir*, p. 1.

83., Ibid., p. 5.

84. Early poems in the *New Age*, under Muir's pseudonym, Edward Moore, as early as 1913, suggest that Muir had begun writing publishable poetry in his late twenties.

correctly, that the criticism and translation are subordinate.[85] However, Butter reminds us that

> He was concerned with the imaginative truth of what a writer conveys, and with details of style only in so far as these are a writer's means of embodying his vision. As we have seen, he thought that criticism could be the starting point for "an inquiry into the human spirit."[86]

In the early poems, Butter comments,

> one feels the presence of strong and genuine emotions struggling for expression, but the words fail in precision.[87]

From the typically descriptive sketches in *First Poems*,[88] Muir moved to the complex *Chorus of the Newly Dead*,[89] and then to the more adequate and realized *Variations on a Time Theme*.[90] Butter sees the themes of the last work centered upon the ideas that, paradoxically, there exist in our sensibilities both a consciousness of mortality and a consciousness of immortality, that we are imprisoned in a forordained length of time while alive, and that we still experience moments of freedom and timelessness. Adding *Journeys and Places*[91] to his list of Muir's less successful works, Butter concludes that it was really in and after *The Narrow Place*[92] in 1943 that Muir extended the range of the poet's powers by looking more to the outward, external world rather than to the imaginative, inner world. He concludes that

---

85. What should be kept in mind by the reader is that the exercise of criticism for Muir was the best means of keeping track of what was happening in literature. At the same time his views have often proved to be highly influential, as well as in most cases essentially correct. I believe there is no well-known modern poet who has left a more adequate record of a concern for the stream of modern imaginative literature, and Muir is unique in terms of the sheer quantity of his critical work centering upon modern developments in English literature.

86. Butter, *Edwin Muir*, p. 36.

87. Ibid., p. 51.

88. *First Poems* (London: Hogarth, 1925).

89. Muir, E., *Chorus of the Newly Dead* (London: Hogarth, 1926).

90. *Variations on a Time Theme* (London: Dent, 1934).

91. *Journeys and Places* (London: Dent, 1937)

92. *The Narrow Place* (London: Faber, 1943).

If he had been able to do nothing but look back and till over and over again the small field of his childhood memories, his inspiration would surely, like Wordsworth's, have dried up. He was to show himself able to assimilate new experiences as well as to achieve clearer understanding of past ones, to look out at the world around him and to apprehend the patterns, revealed in myth, which underlie history.[93]

Keeping in mind what amounts to a kind of metaphysical set of assumptions, we can find in the 1943 book of poems

an advance on what had gone before both in skill and in range. There is a greater mastery of a variety of metrical forms and of rhythmical effects.[94]

The result in future works (from 1943 on) is an illumination of the contemporary experience—an advance on those who know nothing but the fragmentary experience of the present. The earlier poems hinted at invisible, suggestive qualities; but in *The Narrow Place*, the poet has instead embodied the larger significance in appropriate language in the text of the poem itself.

For Butter *The Voyage and other Poems*[95] shows significant accomplishments. First and foremost, one finds a highly accomplished and skillful mastery of the poetic medium. As important as this is Muir's voice, which gives the impression that he is engaging in personal conversation with the reader. There is also an absence of sentimentality, as well as a kind of mature serenity. At this point Butter finds less resistance to reality, and discovers the dominance of a concomitant growth in the attributes of acceptance and gratitude. We find in Muir the attestation of a new kind of knowledge growing to wisdom as a result of the poet's victories over experience. Examining "The Transmutation,"[96] "Time Held in Time's Despite,"[97] "For Ann Scott-Moncrieff (1914–1943),"[98] "A Birthday,"[99] "All

93. Butter, *Edwin Muir*, p. 65.

94. Ibid., p. 67.

95. *The Voyage and other Poems* (London: Faber, 1946).

96. "The Transmutation," pp. 154–155.

97. "Time Held in Time's Despite," p. 155.

98. "For Ann Scott-Moncrieff (1914–1943)," pp. 156–157.

99. "A Birthday," pp. 157–158.

We,"[100] and "In Love for Long,"[101] Butter finds evidence of a philosophic transformation that is not so much the finding of an escape from time, but rather "an escape from the conception of time as a closed circle."[102] The poet does not achieve salvation by dreaming and delineating another world in light of time being a kind of prison; rather he concentrates on developing a profounder vision of that world—as in the case of this group of poems, an exploration is achieved of how "transmutation" works itself out. The "transmutation" occurs in the case of the particular discussed—whether love, friendship, nature, marriage, artistic creation, or a possible deity. With this proliferation of effects, Butter tells us, Muir achieves a kind of wholeness or adequate comprehensibility that is unique and satisfying.

To move on to the poems of The Labyrinth is to find some of Muir's greatest achievements, and, according to Butter, his most consistently high level of accomplishment in the earlier collections. With the newly acquired wisdom that comes with the aging process, the poet was able to look backward most skillfully. Edwin Muir was always searching inward in the imagination and outward in the external environment for patterns; what he found he chose to illustrate by means of myth, dreams, history, and imaginative metaphor. Contrasting the poem "The Labyrinth" with "The Transfiguration,"[103] Butter finds the difference between the nightmare world of the former poem and the "transmutations" and "resurrections" of the latter significant for gaining a comprehension of the duality of Muir's vision—and therefore his continual lack of sentimentality. We sense in the former poem a profound awareness of evil; in the latter "verse artifact," the poet could make a very sharp poetic contrast between a vision of the gods and the threads of history. In another sense, this second poem speaks of these moments when life is entirely holy and significant to humans; this is in sharp contrast to the schizophrenia depicted in "The Labyrinth." For Butter, "The Transfiguration" is equivalent to the idea or ideal of a millennium. Yet Muir never erected a system of belief on the basis of his positive experiences; presumably, he was never that confident about reality. And finally, another poem, "The Combat," reminds us of the sharp contrast between good and evil in the book if the work is taken as a whole. Butter finds that The Labyrinth is imbued with a "luminous simplicity," that

100. "All We," p. 158.

101. "In Love for Long," pp. 159–160.

102. Butter, Edwin Muir, pp. 75–76.

103. "The Transfiguration," pp. 198–200.

"image and theme are more perfectly united," and that the "range and complexity of reference of the symbols is greater" than before.[104]

One Foot in Eden goes beyond particular themes into a scheme for history itself in the opening section. It is a matter of

> a more comprehensive vision of the whole of human history
> than he had attempted before.[105]

The idea of the "resurrection of Christ in the flesh" is seen as a key to the approaches to history in these poems exploring the history of the race, or the "fable." The Christ myth—particularly the motifs of incarnation and transmutation—serve as helpful assumptions for all the poems, in that they add the fabulous element and are seen to serve as a bridge between the real world (or, to put it another way, the eternal world) and the world of history. This is true also with respect to the references to Eden, which are likewise serving something different from ordinary reality, and are thereby relating to something closer to the moments of birth and of death than to real life, as we live it daily. Not only do we find this dualism with respect to the "real world" and the "world beyond worlds"; even within the "world," Muir gives us evidence both in history and in the present moment, according to Butter:

> The perpetually renewed beauty of nature is not presented
> simply as a symbol pointing to something beyond itself; in a
> sense it is Eden, existing now and always,[106]

For Butter, in some of the poems, we come to contemplate the image as eternally present (the *idea* "root," as distinct from just a particular root) and therefore absolute in its implications.

To put it another way, Butter says:

> In Christ the antinomy of flesh and spirit, time and eternity is
> resolved. The Word became flesh, Christ walked the earth as a
> person. The infinite value of each person and the rightness of
> expressing divine mysteries through images are among the
> implications of this.[107]

104. Butter, *Edwin Muir*, p. 87.

105. Ibid.

106. Ibid., p. 89.

107. Ibid., p. 91.

It should be remembered that Butter stresses the fact that in this book, as in the earlier ones, one finds in Muir a variety of types of poems as well as differentiated subject matter.

Turning to the conclusions derived from this semidefinitive examination of the poems, and speaking very generally, Butter finds joy—"the expression of a deep, abiding joy in things that endure"[108] as distinct from a superficial gaiety. He finds significance in the quality of the love poems, and worth in the poems that express his gratitude toward the past. For Butter, Eden is the time of childhood and old age—living in the world (or simply what is called "experience," comes in between these two periods. In Muir's poetry,.according to Butter, there is "a greater sense of wholeness, of tensions having been resolved"[109] than in Yeats. He finds a "pondering on experiences which have been mastered,"[110] and, in light of this, the appropriate "slow and grave and unobtrusive rhythms."[111] As he sees it, the poems

> frequently develop a closely-knit argument; and the bringing-together of a number of thoughts and images into a single sentence helps to show their connexion.[112]

Means are subordinated to ends, and

> the lines glow when charged with strong thought and feeling, as they usually are.[113]

The writing is almost always "austere, competent and uninflated."[114] And finally, it is perhaps most relevant that Muir is able

> to make real some imagined landscape or incident from mythology or dream.[115]

108. Ibid., p. 102.

109. Ibid., p. 105.

110. Ibid., p. 106.

111. Ibid.

112. Ibid., p. 107.

113. Ibid.

114. Ibid., p. 108.

115. Ibid., p. 110.

Muir speaks

> with complete honesty out of his bewilderment as out of his
> faith, and though making something whole and well made in his
> song did not do violence to the mystery of life by claiming to be
> able to contain it in any neat formula.[116]

For Butter, in closing, "the nightmares characteristic of our century are all
present in his poems."[117]

116. Ibid., p. 116.

117. Ibid.

Appendix II: Works Consulted

Blackmur, R. P. "Edwin Muir: Between the Tiger's Paws." *Kenyon Review* 21 (1959), 419–436.

Butter, Peter. *Edwin Muir*. New York: Grove Press, Inc., 1962.

_____. *Edwin Muir: Man and Poet*. Edinburgh: Oliver, 1966.

Daiches, David. *The Novel and the Modern World*. Chicago: University of Chicago Press, 1939.

Empson, William. *Seven Types of Ambiguity*. New York: New Directions, 1947.

Gardner, Helen. *Edwin Muir: The W. D. Thomas Memorial Lecture*. Cardiff: University of Wales, 1961.

Glicksburg, Charles. "Edwin Muir: Zarathustra in Scotch Dress." *Arizona Quarterly* 12 (1956), 225–239.

Grice, Fred. "The Poetry of Edwin Muir." *Essays in Criticism* 5 (1955), 243–252.

Hall, J. C. *Edwin Muir*. In Writers and Their Work, no. 71. London: Longmans, 1956.

Holloway, John. "The Poetry of Edwin Muir." *Hudson Review* 13 (1960–1961), 550–567.

Jennings, Elizabeth. "Edwin Muir as Poet and Allegorist." *London Magazine* 7 (1960), 43–56.

Kafka, Franz, *America*. London: Routledge & Kegan Paul, 1938.[1]

_____. *The Castle*. London: Secker, 1968.

_____. *Description of a Struggle and the Great Wall of China*. London: Secker, 1960.

_____. *In the Penal Settlement: Tales and Short Pieces*. London: Secker, 1948.

_____. *Parables, in German and English*. New York: Schocken Books, Inc., 1959.

_____. *The Penal Colony*. New York: Schocken Books, Inc., 1959.

---

1. All Kafka works listed were translated by the Muirs.

————. *The Trial*. London: Secker, 1968.

Mellown, Elgin. *A Bibliography of the Writings of Edwin Muir*. London: Vane, 1966.

Merton, Thomas. "The True Legendary Sound: The Poetry and Criticism of Edwin Muir." *Sewanee Review* 75 (1967), 317–324.

Muir, Edwin. *An Autobiography*. London: Methuen & Co., Ltd., 1968.

————. *Chorus of the Newly Dead*. London: Hogarth, 1926.

————. *Collected Poems*. New York: Grove Press, Inc., 1957.

————. *Collected Poems*. New York: Oxford University Press, Inc., 1965.

————. *Collected Poems: 1921–1952*. London: Faber & Faber Ltd., 1952.

————. "Correspondences." *Observer* 8422 (2 November 1952), 9.

————. *Essays on Literature and Society*. Boston: Harvard University Press, 1965.

————. *The Estate of Poetry*. Boston: Harvard University Press, 1967.

————. *First Poems*. London: Hogarth, 1925.

————. *Journeys and Places*. London: J. M. Dent & Sons Ltd., 1937.

————. "Labour's Statistical Boa-Constrictor." *New Age* 31 (12 October 1922), 297–298.

————. *The Labyrinth*. London: Faber & Faber Ltd., 1949.

————. *Latitudes*. London: Melrose, 1924.

————. *The Narrow Place*. London: Faber & Faber Ltd., 1943.

————. "A Note on Franz Kafka." *Bookman* (N. Y.) 72 (November 1930), 235–241.

————. *One Foot in Eden*. London: Faber & Faber Ltd., 1956.

————. *Selected Poems*. London: Faber & Faber Ltd., 1965.

————. *Six Poems*. Warlingham: Samson, 1932.

————. "The Status of the Novel." *New Republic* 105 (11 August 1941), 193–195.

————. *The Story and the Fable*. London: Geroge G. Harrap & Co. Ltd., 1940.

————. "The Truth About Art." *Freeman* 4 (15 February 1922), 537–539.

————. *Twentieth Century Poetry in English*. Tape. Washington, D.C.: Library of Congress, 1955.

————. *Variations on a Time Theme*. London: J. M. Dent & Sons Ltd., 1934.

————. "Views and Reviews." *New English Weekly* 8 (31 October 1935), 50–51.

————. *The Voyage and Other Poems*. London: Faber & Faber Ltd., 1946.

————. *We Moderns*. New York: Alfred A. Knopf, Inc., 1920.

Muir, Willa. *Belonging*. London: Hogarth, 1968.

Raine, Kathleen. "Edwin Muir: An Appreciation." *Texas Quarterly* 4 (1961), 233–245.